ENGLISH

KEY STAGE TWO
SCOTTISH LEVELS C-E

POETRY

MOIRA ANDREW

Published by Scholastic Ltd,
Villiers House,
Clarendon Avenue,
Leamington Spa,
Warwickshire CV32 5PR
Text © Moira Andrew
© 1998 Scholastic Ltd
1 2 3 4 5 6 7 8 9 0 8 9 0 1 2 3 4 5 6 7

AUTHOR
MOIRA ANDREW

EDITOR
JOEL LANE

ASSISTANT EDITOR
CLARE MILLER

SERIES DESIGNER
LYNNE JOESBURY

DESIGNER
SARAH ROCK

ILLUSTRATIONS
PAULA MARTYR

COVER ILLUSTRATION
JONATHAN BENTLEY

INFORMATION TECHNOLOGY CONSULTANT
MARTIN BLOWS

SCOTTISH 5–14 LINKS
MARGARET SCOTT AND SUSAN GOW

Designed using Adobe Pagemaker

British Library Cataloguing-in-Publication Data
A catalogue record for this book is available from the
British Library.

ISBN 0-590-53787-3

Contents

ACKNOWLEDGEMENTS

The publishers gratefully acknowledge permission to reproduce the following copyright material:

© **Moira Andrew** for 'Sea seasons', 'Snake', 'Ten things to do with a frisbee', 'Letter from Egypt' and 'Power' all previously unpublished © 1998, Moira Andrew; 'Beyond my house' published in *Dear Future – A Time Capsule of Poems* edited by David Orme © 1998, Moira Andrew (1998, Hodder Children's Books); 'Raspberry jam' and 'One-parent family' from *A Shooting Star* edited by Wes Magee © 1985, Moira Andrew (1985, Basil Blackwell); 'Moon thoughts' from *Marbles In My Pocket* edited by Moira Andrew © 1986, Moira Andrew (1986, Macmillan Educational); 'Poem' from *Go and Open the Door* edited by Moira Andrew © 1987, Moira Andrew (1987, Macmillan Educational); three lines from 'Child with a cause' from *All In the Family* edited by John Foster © 1993, Moira Andrew (1993, OUP); 'Racing the wind' from *Racing the Wind* by Moira Andrew © Moira Andrew (Nelson); 'Nursery rhyme updated' from *Through a Window* edited by Wendy Body © 1995, Moira Andrew (1995, Longman); 'Nature Study' from *Another Fourth Poetry Book* edited by John Foster © 1989, Moira Andrew (1989, OUP).

© **Carcanet Press** for the use of 'The Alice Jean' by Robert Graves from *The Magic Tree – Complete Poems* by Robert Graves, edited by David Woolger © 1981, Robert Graves (1981, OUP).

© **Andrew Collett** for the use of 'No excuses' from *Whoops Pyjamas!* by Andrew Collett © 1997, Andrew Collett (1997, Poetry In Performance Press).

© **John Cotton** for the use of 'Through that door' from *Two By Two* by John Cotton and Fred Sedgwick © 1990, John Cotton (1990, Mary Glasgow) and four lines from 'Aunt Flo' by John Cotton from *Over the Bridge* edited by John Loveday © 1981, John Cotton (1981, Puffin).

© **Richard Edwards** for the use of 'Sunlight or surprise?' from *Whispers From a Wardrobe* by Richard Edwards © 1987, Richard Edwards (1987, Lutterworth Press) and four lines from 'Don't' from *The Word Party* by Richard Edwards © 1986, Richard Edwards (1986, Lutterworth Press).

© **Faber & Faber** for 'Biking' by Judith Nicholls from *Midnight Forest* by Judith Nicholls © 1987, Judith Nicholls (1987, Faber & Faber).

© **Michael Harrison** for 'Monday' from *Junk Mail* by Michael Harrison © 1993, Michael Harrison (1993, OUP).

© **David Higham Associates** for 'Miller's End' by Charles Causley from *Collected Poems 1951–75* by Charles Causley © 1975, Charles Causley (1975, Macmillan).

© **Mike Johnson** for the use of 'Poetree' by Mike Johnson from *Poetry Street* by David Orme and James Sale © 1990, Mike Johnson (1990, Longman).

© **John Loveday** for the use of 'A driftwood pendant' by John Loveday from *Particular Sunlights* by John Loveday © 1986, John Loveday (1986, Headland Publications).

© **Wes Magee** for 'The house on the hill' from *Morning Break and Other Poems* by Wes Magee © 1989, Wes Magee (1989, CUP).

© **Judith Nicholls** for 'Night' from *Magic Mirror* by Judith Nicholls © 1993 Judith Nicholls (1993, Faber & Faber), first published in *Marbles In My Pocket* edited by Moira Andrew © 1986, Judith Nicholls (1986, Macmillan); for the use of 'What can you do with a pencil?' from *Storm's Eye* by Judith Nicholls © 1994, Judith Nicholls (1994, OUP); and for four lines from 'Grandpa' from *Wish You Were Here?* by Judith Nicholls © 1992, Judith Nicholls (1992, OUP).

© **Parvin Rieu** for the use of 'The paintbox' by E.V. Rieu from *The First Lick of the Lolly* edited by Moira Andrew © 1986, E.V. Rieu (1986, Macmillan).

© **Vernon Scannell** for the use of 'The apple raid' from *The Apple Raid* by Vernon Scannell © 1974, Vernon Scannell (1974, Chatto & Windus).

© **The Watts Group** for the use of 'Rebbit rap' by Tony Mitton from *Royal Rap* by Tony Mitton © 1996, Tony Mitton (1996, Orchard Books, a division of The Watts Publishing Group, 96 Leonard Street, London EC2A 4HR).

Introduction

Scholastic Curriculum Bank is a series for all primary teachers, providing an essential planning tool for devising comprehensive schemes of work as well as an easily accessible and varied bank of practical, classroom-tested activities with photocopiable resources.

Designed to help planning for and implementation of progression, differentiation and assessment, *Scholastic Curriculum Bank* offers a structured range of stimulating activities with clearly stated learning objectives that reflect the programmes of study, and detailed lesson plans that allow busy teachers to put ideas into practice with the minimum amount of preparation time. The photocopiable sheets that accompany many of the activities provide ways of integrating purposeful application of knowledge and skills, differentiation, assessment and record-keeping.

Opportunities for formative assessment are highlighted within the activities where appropriate, and a useful checklist for assessing the children's writing, reading and listening is provided on page 12. Ways of using information technology for different purposes and in different contexts, as a tool for communicating and handling information and as a means of investigating, are integrated into the activities where appropriate, and more explicit guidance is provided at the end of the book.

The series covers all the primary curriculum subjects, with separate books for Key Stages 1 and 2 or Scottish Levels A–B and C–E. It can be used as a flexible resource with any scheme, to fulfil National Curriculum and Scottish 5–14 requirements and to provide children with a variety of different learning experiences that will lead to effective acquisition of skills and knowledge.

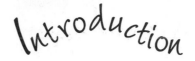

SCHOLASTIC CURRICULUM BANK POETRY

The *Scholastic Curriculum Bank English* books enable teachers to plan comprehensive and structured coverage of the primary English curriculum, and enable pupils to develop the required skills, knowledge and understanding through activities.

Each book covers one key stage. There are six books for Key Stage 1/Scottish levels A–B and six for Key Stage 2/Scottish levels C–E. These books reflect the programme of study for English, so that there are titles on Reading, Writing, Speaking and listening, and Spelling and phonics. The titles on Poetry and Drama cover all four aspects of the programme of study in relation to these subjects.

Bank of activities
This book provides a bank of activities which are designed to broaden children's experience of poetry and enable them to develop their ability to listen effectively, to read with understanding and to write confidently using a range of poetic forms and techniques.

Lesson plans
Detailed lesson plans, under clear headings, are given for each activity and provide material for immediate implementation in the classroom. The structure for each activity is as follows:

Activity title box
The information contained in the box at the beginning of each activity outlines the following key aspects:

▲ *Activity title and learning objective.* For each activity, a clearly stated learning objective is given in bold italics. These learning objectives break down aspects of the programmes of study for English and the National Literacy Strategy *Framework for Teaching* into manageable, hierarchical teaching and learning chunks, and their purpose is to aid planning for progression. These objectives can easily be referenced to the National Curriculum and Scottish 5–14 requirements by using the overview grid on pages 13–16.

▲ *Class organization/Likely duration.* Icons ♯♯ and ⏰ signpost the suggested group sizes for each activity and the approximate amount of time required to complete it.

Previous skills/knowledge needed
Information is given here when it is necessary for the children to have acquired specific knowledge or skills prior to carrying out the activity.

Key background information
The information in this section outlines the areas of study covered by each activity and gives a general background to the particular topic or theme, outlining the basic skills that will be developed and the way in which the activity will address children's learning.

Preparation
Advice is given for those occasions when it is necessary for the teacher to prime the pupils for the activity or to prepare materials, or to set up a display or activity ahead of time.

Resources needed
All materials needed to carry out the activity are listed, so that the pupils or the teacher can gather them together easily before the beginning of the teaching session.

What to do
Easy-to-follow, step-by-step instructions are given for carrying out the activity, including (where appropriate) suggested questions for the teacher to ask pupils to help instigate discussion and stimulate investigation.

Suggestion(s) for extension/support
In these sections, ideas are given for ways of providing easy differentiation. Suggestions are provided as to ways in which each activity can be modified for less able or extended for more able children.

Assessment opportunities
Where appropriate, opportunities for ongoing teacher assessment of the children's work during or after a specific activity are highlighted.

Opportunities for IT
Where opportunities for IT present themselves, these are briefly outlined with reference to particularly suitable types of program. The chart on page 159 presents specific areas of IT covered in the activities, together with more detailed support on how to apply particular types of program. Selected lesson plans serve as models for other activities by providing more comprehensive guidance on the application of IT; these lesson plans are indicated by bold page numbers on the grid and the [icon] icon at the start of the activity.

Display/performance ideas
Where they are relevant and innovative, display ideas are incorporated into activity plans and illustrated with examples. For many poetry activities, a performance may be an appropriate outcome rather than (or as well as) a display. In these cases, a range of performance activities is suggested.

Reference to photocopiable sheets
Where activities include photocopiable activity sheets, small reproductions of these are included in the lesson plans together with guidance notes for their use and, where appropriate, suggested answers.

Assessment
Assessment of children's work on poetry includes specific assessment of reading, writing, and speaking and listening. Assessment of speaking and listening may be more subjective than assessment of reading and writing; but it is still important to make a careful assessment and keep records of attainment. Each activity includes suggestions for formative assessment, and some can be used for a more formal, summative assessment of progress.

Photocopiable sheets
Many of the activities are accompanied by photocopiable sheets. For some activities, the sheet is a resource (usually a poem) which the teacher can use in various specific ways within the activity, often providing differentiation by task. Other sheets are used for recording, or for relatively open-ended tasks, in order to provide differentiation by outcome. The photocopiable sheets provide purposeful activities that are ideal for assessment and can be kept as records in pupils' portfolios of work.

Cross-curricular links
Cross-curricular links are identified on a simple grid (see page 160) which cross-references the activities in each chapter to the programmes of study for other subjects in the curriculum, suggesting possible links between the activities and work in other subject areas.

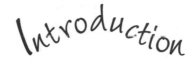

POETRY AT KEY STAGE 2

Poetry allows us to use language in exciting and imaginative ways. Because poetry can move, excite or amuse us, it brings a personal element to any curriculum area in which it is used.

Reading poetry aloud and listening to it can be a valuable shared experience. To make this possible for the children, it is important that teachers make anthologies and collections of poetry readily accessible in the classroom. They should take time to read poems to the children, choosing from a wide variety of authors, styles and cultures.

Children should be encouraged to respond in various ways to the poems which they have read or heard. They may want to talk about the poems, to draw and paint in response or to present their own interpretation through drama. However, their most important response is in writing their own poems. In doing this, they should use patterns and structures which allow them to explore and experiment with language – and thus, crucially, to find and follow the approaches which give them success as writers.

Children like poems. They enjoy reading and listening to them, and will often choose a poetry anthology rather than a story book from the library shelves. This should come as no surprise: a child can read an entire poem in a snatched moment between two lessons, or just before the bell rings for playtime. It is difficult to do the same thing with a story!

A wide variety of poetry books should be made accessible to the children, so that they can find their own favourite poems, listen to the music of the words in their heads and paint pictures in their imagination. The children should learn to appreciate the patterns that words can make on the page, and look for unfamiliar poems to read for themselves.

Most children enjoy hearing and reading old favourites time after time – think, for example, of the continuing popularity of traditional nursery rhymes with young children. Children have a natural ear for rhythm and rhyme. Of course, though all poems have an element of rhythm, they don't need to rhyme; this idea should be reinforced, especially if children are having problems with their own work. There is nothing less desirable than the forced rhymes which children (and adults) feel obliged to produce when they think that 'a poem must rhyme'.

Poetry is a way of playing with words. When they come to school, young children already have some experience of word-play through jokes, limericks, TV jingles and playground chants. No child comes to school as a raw recruit to poetry.

The Literacy Hour

The National Literacy Strategy suggests that achieving better standards in literacy depends on establishing a closer connection between reading and writing. This book – and

its companion volume, *Curriculum Bank Poetry (Key Stage 1)* – highlight this principle. The activities are designed to fit the proposed Literacy Hour, give or take ten minutes or so. Most of the activities follow the procedure recommended by the National Literacy Strategy: whole-class work with some direct teaching input, followed by group, paired or individual reading, writing and/or discussion.

Many of these activities are introduced by whole-class work: either listening to poems read aloud by the teacher, or class reading and discussion orchestrated by the teacher. Often, it is suggested that the teacher incorporate some of the children's ideas into a piece of class writing on a flip chart or whiteboard; this writing can then be used as part of the reading repertoire in the classroom.

The recommendations for the Literacy Hour also state that the children should be questioned to probe their understanding. The activities in this book suggest questions which will help children to reflect on their own work, and to extend and explore their ideas about published poems and their authors.

There is ample opportunity in the design of these activities to encourage discussion among the children, leading them to evaluate their own and other children's work. Where appropriate, it is suggested that the teacher stimulate and guide the children's language play (as recommended in the National Literacy Strategy).

In order to develop children's writing, we have included poems which provide structures, themes and ideas which children are invited to consider and to use as a pattern for their own work. The activities suggest that many of the writing patterns and structures be modelled by the teacher (from the children's suggestions) before the children work on them independently.

Emphasis is also placed on developing the children's skills in planning, drafting and editing their own poems. Finally, still within the Literacy Hour, it should be possible for many of the children to share their work with others in the class. Follow-up work on display of the children's poems in handwritten or word-processed form is also important, as is the idea that performance can bring another dimension to the children's written work.

Listening to poems

Poetry is for sharing, and the most effective way of sharing is to read poems aloud to groups of children or to the whole class. Listening sessions should be as varied, interesting and exciting as possible. The children should be encouraged to take an active part in these sessions. Active listening implies choosing, discussing, questioning and evaluating the poems.

As a rule, poetry is written to be heard; so many of the activities in this book start with a class listening session. The teacher must decide whether it is better to plunge straight into a given poem with no preliminary remarks or

to 'set the scene' before reading. Prior explanation can help children to engage with the poem when they hear it and save them 'getting lost'; but it may also diminish the effect of mystery and surprise.

In regular listening sessions, the teacher should introduce a range of poetic styles: rhyming and non-rhyming; narrative and descriptive poems; verse/chorus and other patterns; poems to make the children think, to make them feel different emotions and to make them laugh.

Children enjoy playing with language. That is how they learn what language can do – as description, as persuasion and as instruction. Listening to the ways that different poets make language work for them helps children to develop their own language skills, and to deepen and extend their vocabulary.

Classroom anthologies

The compilation of classroom anthologies of poetry gives children the opportunity to make choices for themselves. They should be encouraged to browse through published collections and anthologies of poetry, recognizing different themes and styles (humorous poems, narrative poems and so on). They should look at the patterning of words on the page, and listen to the rhythms of words read aloud. Each anthology can be compiled by an individual or a group. It can include a mixture of previously published material and children's own work.

When the children have selected their favourite poems, they should be able to give simple and clear explanations of the reasons for their choices. Encourage them to copy out their chosen poems in 'best' handwriting, or to use a word processor. They can add written comments about why they like (or don't like) these poems. It is a good idea for them to leave enough room for others in the class to add their comments (both positive and negative), so that the book incorporates its own review.

Classroom anthologies offer a unique opportunity to stress the importance of clear, neat presentation in communicating the meaning of a text effectively. The books can be illustrated in pen and ink (which is ideal for photocopying), in coloured pencil or in felt-tipped pen. The children can draw appropriate borders around the poems. If older children are producing an anthology for the younger children in the school, it could be made up into a large floor book.

Compiling and producing classroom anthologies can be a valuable aspect of topic work – for example, gathering together poems about travel, the weather or school. Anthologies can also be devised to help children learn about different kinds of poems by choosing examples of narrative poems, riddles, acrostics, haiku and so on.

Children as writers

Poetry is an ideal way of practising the process of writing. It helps the writer (whether child or adult) to express thoughts and feelings in a clear and economical way. The poem format encourages us to make every word work for its place.

Children with learning difficulties are often very enthusiastic about writing poetry. Of course, a poem need not be long; and writing poems can be more fun than writing prose. Following a simple repetitive pattern usually brings success!

Teaching strategies

The following strategies are worth keeping in mind when teaching children to write poetry.

Brainstorming and listing

A tried-and-tested way of starting direct teacher input into children's poetry-writing is, following a discussion session, to scribe the children's suggestions on the flip chart or board. This can take the form of 'brainstorming' (also known as 'blitzing'): writing down all the children's responses as they come up with them on a wheel, spider or tree diagram (see illustration below). Such a diagram allows trains of thought and relationships between words to be displayed immediately.

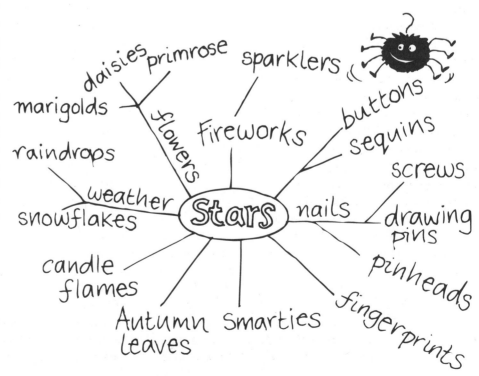

One disadvantage of brainstorming is that it is not always easy for the less confident child to make sense of the profusion of words and phrases on the board. Another is that, while acting as scribe, the teacher needs to remain conscious of children on the periphery of the class and encourage them to take part – which is difficult in a quick-fire 'say and scribe' session.

As an alternative , it is sometimes more effective to make a linear 'shopping list' of ideas under headings. This makes it easier for the slower children to read the words scribed on the board and choose the ones they want.

Word-trading

When acting as scribe for the children, the teacher should avoid the easy option of simply letting the children think aloud and writing down whatever they say. A useful strategy to prompt their thinking is to 'trade words' with them orally: building vocabulary word on word until a 'word stack' is available to them. For example, in building a stack of words to describe the movement of a boat, the children can be encouraged to work from 'sailing' to 'floating', 'bobbing', 'rocking', 'skimming' and so on. This strategy allows the teacher and children to explore the richness of our language.

Following a brainstorming/listing session, the teacher can use many of the children's suggestions to create a class poem – either by writing a poem using the listed words or by collaborating with the class in composing a poem. This will help to develop the children's confidence and writing skills. In addition, word-trading helps to demonstrate the process of building a poem, especially where a specific structure or pattern has been suggested.

Patterns and structures

It is a mistake to assume that the use of a poetic structure or pattern will necessarily inhibit a child's imagination. There is nothing more inhibiting, for a child or an adult, than to be presented with a blank piece of paper and asked to 'write a poem about Spring' (or whatever). This is a passport to failure. Working to the discipline of a given poetic format, on the other hand, often frees the child to concentrate on images, descriptions and comparisons. Poems are a way of fitting words into patterns; and working within a given form allows children to experience the excitement of

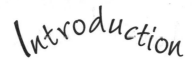

making words and ideas fit together like a jigsaw. There is no need to impose difficult formal restrictions on children who are unready for them: a basic structure such as a verse/chorus pattern or a haiku is easy to learn and use.

Planning, drafting and editing

The process of planning, drafting and editing – going from 'rough' work to 'best' – offers children a working strategy for any form of writing. Writing poems is perhaps the best way to learn the process of drafting, one of the essential skills of a writer. The words in a poem have to be well-chosen and some may have to be rejected, so this is an ideal place to start; and because poems are usually fairly short, children are not too daunted by the task.

To demonstrate the process of planning, the teacher should work from the original brainstorming/listing session, developing ideas from the flip chart across several sheets of paper. Children are generally most impressed to see the teacher cross out words and whole phrases, use arrows and generally make a mess of the first few drafts. *Think about the pattern of the poem. Will it be a number poem? Will it rhyme? Will it be a simple 'snapshot'? Or should it be a freewheeling poem?* Explore the options with the children as you go along.

When a pattern has been decided upon, suggest that it might be useful to come up with a good opening line. Ask the children for suggestions. If the poem is describing an old broken watch, for example, possible first lines might be:

The watch had stopped, but time ticked on...
Times past, hands broken, memories forgotten...
Who once owned this mystery watch?...
Hundreds of hours, millions of minutes...

Don't spend too much time on this exercise. Choose an opening line fairly quickly, but don't discard the other suggestions: they might well fit somewhere else in the poem at a later stage. Begin to build up a draft of the poem, line by line – perhaps moving words and phrases around, adding here, deleting there. Having second thoughts is a necessary part of drafting.

As you begin the final editing process, try to explain how you are making choices: looking for the most striking image, taking out unnecessary words, looking at line endings and punctuation, checking the rhythm, and so on. Gradually, with assistance from the children, a finished poem should emerge from the scribbled word lists and drafts.

At last, on the final sheet, a poem is born! This can be a slow and tiring process; but you should try to convey to the children how satisfying it is to arrive at a finished piece, ready to be copied out and displayed to best advantage. When the children have watched their teacher at work, it gives them confidence that they can use the same process: that crossings-out, arrows, rethinks and changes of all kinds are acceptable. Encourage the children to work through the process themselves: from brainstorming to planning, drafting, and finally editing.

The National Curriculum documents stress the importance of drafting. Under 'Key Skills' in the Programme of Study for English at Key Stage 2, it is stated that 'Pupils should have opportunities to plan and review their writing, assembling and developing their ideas on paper and on screen.' Many of the activities in this book include drafting and revising as a matter of course, even if these processes are not specifically highlighted in the learning objective.

Teachers are often uncertain how much help children should be offered at the drafting stage, and organizing this support can be a major problem for literacy work in the classroom. The following strategies will help to minimise the demands made on teacher time:

▲ If the children have been encouraged to review and revise their own work (following the process outlined above) from early on, they should be able to tackle the creation of a first draft for themselves.

▲ When working on a draft with individual children, the teacher should look for no more than two points (such as 'finding a better word' and 'listening to the rhythm').

▲ Children can sometimes work together (in groups or pairs) to create a draft.

▲ If a common problem arises, discuss it with the class. *'Can we all think how to help Gemma? She is stuck with a rhyme for...'*

▲ Give positive feedback by saying which part(s) of a poem you particularly like. Confidence is an important part of creativity!

Children who are used to the drafting process don't view the teacher's input as 'marking'. They want their work to look as good as possible when it is displayed, and are happy to receive help and advice. When all the hard work of drafting and editing has been completed, there is a feeling of euphoria. The children can now look forward to presenting their poems as attractively as possible.

Presentation

Imaginative displays of children's work are an important feature of the primary school environment. Such displays – arranged with care and attention to detail – both reinforce learning and demonstrate to the children that their work is valued by the adults in the school.

There are many interesting ways to display children's poetry: framed poems, one-poem books, zig-zag books, poems written inside flaps and opening doors, poetry mobiles and sculptures, class poems displayed on a backing frieze, and so on. The teacher should try to vary the form of writing: sometimes using italic pens, sometimes a word processor (with a variety of different fonts). The poems can be illustrated by paint, collage, felt-tipped pen or coloured pencil. Sometimes a black and white display is best for the topic; at other times, black and silver or black and gold may work better.

Where possible, encourage the children to make their own choices – especially when it comes to adding books, pottery, plants and so on to a finished display.

Performance

The children should be encouraged to read aloud their own and other people's poems. Help them to use their voices effectively: changing pace, using appropriate stresses and pauses, and so on. This practice is emphasized throughout the book.

When the children have read and listened to poems, they should be given the opportunity to respond to them and present them through a range of drama activities. They will enjoy bringing the poems to life through role-play and improvisation, often using simple props (hats, cloaks, swords and so on). They can enact the stories of narrative poems, such as 'The *Alice Jean*' by Robert Graves (see 'Tell me a story', page 38).

The children should also be encouraged to present their own poems, on tape or to a live audience, in the form of a play or improvisation. Sometimes their poems can be set to music, using a piano, violin or percussion instruments. Where poems have a lively beat, children can sing the words.

Another dramatic way of performing poems to an audience is choral speaking. This needs a lot of rehearsal, but can be very effective. A musical backing can be provided, either played live or pre-recorded.

As recommended in the National Literacy Strategy, the children should be encouraged to evaluate their own and others' performance of poetry.

Writer's notebook

The children should be encouraged to keep a 'writer's notebook' to record useful words, phrases and ideas. Things they might look out for include:

▲ Colour, sound or movement words which they have found in a poem, a story or even an advert, and which appeal to them. Source is no guarantee of excellence.

▲ Snatches of overheard conversation or particular words which epitomize the way different people (such as a grandparent or a baby sister) talk.

▲ Observations and images that occur to them – for example, *The new moon is like a Rich Tea biscuit with a bite taken out of it.*

These notes will be useful at a later date, and the process of keeping a notebook reinforces an essential aspect of creativity: remembering things for later reference. Most adult poets keep 'ideas' notebooks.

The imaginative leap

Although pattern and structure can be important in starting children off on poetry-writing (see above), the ability to take an unconventional *'sideways look'* at everyday things is

what goes to make a genuine poet. Children who show that they can make such imaginative leaps should be supported and encouraged. The teacher should always be on the lookout for children whose work has the indefinable *'tingle factor'*, the ability to send a shiver down the spine. These are the poets of the future!

Assessment

The best poetry takes the reader by surprise – and this characteristic makes it very difficult to assess or grade 'out of ten'. There are no fully satisfactory objective criteria against which to judge poetry-writing. However, there are some questions that the teacher can consider in making an assessment of a child's poem:

▲ Does the poem cast a new and surprising light on its subject?

▲ Has the writer made good and appropriate choices of language?

▲ Is the grammar correct (for example, no change of tense halfway through the poem)?

▲ Is the punctuation correct?

▲ Does every word count, with nothing unnecessary or repeated (except for repetitions that are part of a poem's structure)?

▲ How do the other children feel about the poem?

▲ How does the writer feel about the poem?

▲ Did you feel a 'tingle' or 'shiver' when you read it?

Children's responses to poems read aloud are even more difficult to assess, but there are some questions that you can keep in mind:

▲ Do the children listen with interest and concentration, keeping quiet and still while listening?

▲ Can they answer literal questions about the poem?

▲ Are they able to explore, develop and explain ideas about the content of the poem?

▲ Are they sensitive to the feelings expressed in the poem?

▲ Can they predict what might happen next after the end of a narrative poem?

▲ Can they share ideas and insights with others in the class or group?

▲ Are they eager to take part in further poetry-listening sessions?

▲ Do they want to hear particular poems reread, and can they say why?

When children are reading poetry for themselves, consider the following questions:

▲ Do they read poems for pleasure?

▲ Are they interested in reading a range of poetry, not simply the most 'fun' poems?

▲ Do they understand and appreciate the use of images, including similes and metaphors?

▲ Do they show an interest in 'classic' poetry?

▲ Are they interested in poems from other cultures?

▲ Can they 'get lost' in a poetry book?

Title	Learning objective	PoS/AO	Content	Type of activity	Page
Listening and reading					
Listening for clues	To listen to a poem and discuss it. To be aware of how a poet's choice of words and phrases creates a particular impression.	Speaking and listening 1a, c; 3b. Reading 1b, c. *Listening in groups, Level C.*	Encouraging the children to look for clues 'hidden' in the language of a poem in order to establish effective listening.	Reading/listening and discussion with whole class (or group of six to ten children).	18
I got rhythm, I got rap	To consolidate listening skills. To develop a sense of rhythm and rhyme through clapping out and counting the syllables of a poem. To draft and write out a poem, then rehearse and perform it with percussion accompaniment.	Speaking and listening 1a, d; 2a; 3b. Writing 1a, b; 2b. *Awareness of genre, Level C.*	Developing a sense of rhythm, with some work on rhyming words.	Reading/listening with whole class, then writing/speaking in pairs or small groups (up to six).	20
Rhyme time	To think about the sound of the words used in poems. To develop an understanding of rhyming words and rhyming patterns by reading and writing short poems that use rhyme.	Speaking and listening 1a, d; 2a, b; 3b. Reading 1a, d. Writing 1a, b, c; 2d. *Knowledge about language, Level B.*	Understanding and exploring rhyme patterns by listening to and making up short rhyming poems.	Reading/listening with whole class, then writing/speaking in groups; reading/listening with whole class, then writing individually.	24
Tricky rhymes	To practise listening for and using words that rhyme in less obvious ways, including near-rhymes or half-rhymes.	Speaking and listening 1a, c, d; 2a; 3a, b. Reading 1a. Writing 1c. *As above.*	Listening for and using more difficult rhymes and rhyming patterns.	Whole-class introduction, then group writing.	27
The house on the hill	To develop the capacity for sustained listening. To explore, explain and share ideas on how a poem is constructed. To respond to a poem through imaginative role play and a class reading.	Speaking and listening 1a, d; 2a, b. Reading 1a. *Listening in order to respond to text, Level C.*	Developing sustained listening skills by looking at and listening to the way in which a poem is written and poetic devices are used.	Whole-class introduction, then role play and oral composition (scribed by the teacher) in four groups.	29
Family album	To listen with care to a poem in order to explore the use of descriptive and figurative language. To compare and contrast poems on similar themes. To use photographs and published poems as stimuli for writing descriptive poems.	Speaking and listening 1a, b, d. Reading 1c. Writing 1a, 2b. *Awareness of genre, Level D.*	Exploring the way in which character can be conveyed in a poem and contrasting poems on a specific theme. Listening and writing.	Whole-class reading/listening, discussion and group writing, then individual writing.	32
Portraits of summer	To develop the ability to listen with care to a poem and evaluate it, going on to compare and contrast poems on a similar theme and respond to them through discussion. To identify clues which suggest that a poem was written in a previous generation.	Speaking and listening 1a, b, c, d; 2a, b. Reading 1c, d. *Listening in order to respond to text, Level D.*	Listening and responding to poems which were written in a previous generation.	Whole-class reading/listening and discussion.	35
Tell me a story	To experience poetry as narrative through listening to, reading and discussing a range of narrative poems.	Speaking and listening 1a, b, d; 2a, b. Reading 1a, c, d; 2b. Writing 2a (extension). *As above.*	Listening and responding to poems written as narrative; looking for other narrative poems.	Reading/listening and discussion as a whole class and as three groups.	38

POETRY

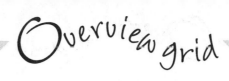
Title	Learning objective	PoS/AO	Content	Type of activity	Page
Old Jack Rags	To listen to a poem being read aloud and to analyse how the poem conveys a message, feelings and attitudes. To discuss their opinions on the poem's content.	Speaking and listening 1a, b, d; 2a, b; 3a. Reading 1a, c, d. Writing 1a, c; 2a, b. *Listening in order to respond to text, Level D.*	Listening and discussing the content of a poem which makes the reader think about the truth or otherwise of 'things people say'. Writing responses.	Whole-class reading/ listening and discussion, then group and individual writing.	41
One-parent family	To look at how a character is presented in a poem. To develop personal responses to the poem through discussion of the issues and attitudes which the poem addresses.	Speaking and listening 1a, c; 2a, b; 3a, b. Reading 1a, d; 2b, c. *As above.*	Looking critically at the perceived ideas of a family unit through detailed exploration of a poem.	Whole-class discussion, group discussion, whole-class reading/listening, then group writing.	44

Writing poems

Title	Learning objective	PoS/AO	Content	Type of activity	Page
Images of the moon	To generate ideas by brainstorming, and go on to draft poems. To use simile and metaphor in poetry writing.	Speaking and listening 1a, b; 2a, b. Reading 1a, d. Writing 1a, b; 2b. *Knowledge about language, Level E.*	Working through the process of making up a poem, based on a writing pattern which uses simile.	Whole-class modelling, then individual writing.	48
A poem is...	To write verses for a group poem based on a repetitive starting point.	Speaking and listening 1a; 2a, b. Reading 1c. Writing 1a; 2b. *Imaginative writing, Level D.*	Writing definition poems, from a brainstorming session to individual work.	Whole-class modelling, group writing, then individual writing.	51
Colour me blue	To use descriptive images of colour in a poem to evoke a mood.	Speaking and listening 1a, b. Writing 1a, c; 2b. *As above.*	Shared writing sessions which develop the idea of using colours to evoke different feelings.	Paired writing, then individual writing.	54
What can I do with it?	To develop the ability to write imaginatively, using observation and figurative language. To consolidate the ideas of simile and metaphor.	Speaking and listening 1a, d. Reading 1a, c; 2a. Writing 1a, c; 2b. *Imaginative writing, Level E.*	Shared writing sessions leading to imaginative descriptive writing which uses simile and metaphor.	Whole-class introduction, writing in groups of six, then individual writing.	56
A river of words	To explore word associations. To experiment with the sounds of words – including rhyme, rhythm and cadence – in order to produce a polished poem through redrafting.	Speaking and listening 1a, b; 2a, b. Writing 1a, c; 2b. *As above.*	Exploring word associations, leading to the drafting and redrafting of a finished poem.	Whole-class oral game, paired writing, then individual writing.	59
Beach-comber	To develop powers of description through careful choice of words and phrases, combining observation and imaginative use of language.	Speaking and listening 1a, d; 2a. Reading 1b, d. Writing 2a, b, c. *As above.*	Developing a finished poem through the use of imaginative descriptive language.	Whole-class modelling, then paired or individual writing.	62
I've found a poem!	To develop a poem through stages of construction and redrafting.	Speaking and listening 1a, c; 2a, b; 3b. Reading 1b. Writing 1a, c; 2b. *As above.*	Writing a poem which used 'found' language from a variety of non-fiction texts.	Whole-class modelling, then individual writing.	65
Box of dreams	To write a 'found' poem, building on a non-fiction text.	Speaking and listening 1a, c. Reading 1a. Writing 1a, b, c; 2b. *Imaginative writing, Level D.*	Drafting and writing a poem using listing techniques and descriptive language from the senses.	Whole-class discussion and modelling, group discussion, then group or individual writing.	68

Title	Learning objective	PoS/AO	Content	Type of activity	Page
Contrasts	To write a poem in response to a specific stimulus, using images derived from sensory experience and paying particular attention to rhythm.	Speaking and listening 1a, b, c; 2a, b. Reading 1b, c; 2a, b. Writing 1a, c; 2b. *Personal writing, Level E.*	Drafting and developing poems based on serious concerns and the idea of contrast (for example, 'war and peace').	Whole-class modelling, then individuals writing in pairs.	70
King am I!	To use expressive language to convey serious personal thoughts and concerns. To produce and redraft poems individually.	Speaking and listening 1a, c; 2a, b; 3b. Reading 1a, b, d. Writing 1a, c; 2b. *Imaginative writing, Level E.*	Writing a fantasy poem which uses descriptive and imaginative language.	Whole-class reading/ listening and discussion, group reading aloud, whole-class shared writing, then individual writing.	73

Using a pattern

Title	Learning objective	PoS/AO	Content	Type of activity	Page
Through that door	To write a fantasy poem in a free style, using rhythm but not rhyme. To use descriptive language in an imaginative context.	Speaking and listening 1a; 2a, b; 3b. Reading 1b, c; 2b. Writing 1a, b, c; 2b. *Awareness of genre, Level C.*	Writing a descriptive poem based on the pattern of a published poem.	Reading/listening and shared writing with the whole class or a large group (at least six), then individual writing.	78
If I were an artist	To listen for and discuss rhyme. To write a descriptive poem based on the rhyme scheme of a published poem.	Speaking and listening 1a; 3b. Reading 1b, d; 2c. Writing 1a, b, c; 2b; 3b, c. *Imaginative writing, Level C.*	Writing a descriptive fantasy poem which uses the structure of a published poem.	Whole-class modelling, then individual writing.	80
Above and beyond	To use the pattern of form and content in a published poem as a basis for imaginative writing.	Speaking and listening 1a; 2a, b; 3a, b. Reading 1a, c. Writing 1a, c; 2b; 3b. *As above.*	Writing a descriptive poem which relies on the use of prepositions and teaches children to look for rhythm.	Whole-class discussion, then individual writing.	82
Inside my head	To use a range of different prepositions as a basis for a descriptive and imaginative poem.	Speaking and listening 1a, c; 2a, b; 3a, b. Reading 1a, c. Writing 1a, b, c; 2b; 3c. *Imaginative writing, Level D.*	Encouraging children to listen to the content of a published poem with a magical quality, and – through drafting and redrafting – to produce a finished piece based on its structure.	Whole-class modelling and shared writing, then individual writing.	84
Recipe for summer	To write an imaginative poem using a published poem as a model. To develop awareness of the evocative qualities of a published poem. To produce a polished final poem through drafting and revising.	Speaking and listening 1a, b; 3b. Reading 1b, c. Writing 1a, b, c; 2b. *As above.*	Moving from a shared listing technique to the composition of a poem which uses the form and language of a recipe.	Whole-class modelling, then individual writing.	88
Alphabet poems	To write a poem within the framework of a recipe. To use descriptive language, including similes.	Speaking and listening 1a; 2a; 3a, b. Reading 1c; 2a, c. Writing 1a, b, c; 2b. *As above.*	Writing poems based on the sequence of the alphabet and a knowledge of alliteration.	Whole-class modelling, then individual writing.	90
Letter poems	To use the alphabet as a structure around which to build a poem. To recognize and use alliteration.	Speaking and listening 1a, c, d; 2a, b; 3a. Reading 1a, c. Writing 1a, b, c; 2a, b. *Imaginative writing, Level E.*	Writing imaginative poems based on the format of a letter.	Whole-class introduction, paired writing, then individual writing.	92

Title	Learning objective	PoS/AO	Content	Type of activity	Page
Playing with forms					
Turnabout poems	To empathize with the feelings of a character and communicate these by writing a letter in the form of a poem.	Speaking and listening 1a, c, d; 3b. Writing 1a, c; 2a, b. *Imaginative writing, Level E.*	Writing poems that use the power of strong verbs, which are not necessarily connected in a direct way to the content.	Whole-class introduction, then individual writing.	96
Haiku	To develop a wide vocabulary of dramatic expressions, and use them in writing poetry.	Speaking and listening 1a, b, c; 2a, b; 3b. Reading 1c, d. Writing 1a, c; 2b; 3b. *Personal writing and Imaginative writing, Level E.*	Understanding and writing poems using the syllabic count and pattern of a haiku.	Whole-class introduction, writing in groups of three, then individual writing.	98
Riddles	To appreciate the haiku form and to write poems in that form, selecting the words carefully.	Speaking and listening 1a, b, c; 2a, b; 3b. Reading 1a, c, d. Writing 1a, c; 2a, b; 3b. *Imaginative writing, Level E.*	Understanding and writing poems in the form of riddles.	Whole-class introduction, writing in pairs or groups, then individual writing.	100
Acrostics	To explore 'riddle' poems and identify their typical features. To write their own riddle poems for a peer audience.	Speaking and listening 1a; 2a, b; 3b. Reading 1d; 2a, b. Writing 1a, c; 2b. *Imaginative writing, Level D/E.*	Recognizing and understanding an acrostic, and writing poems which use this pattern.	Group listing, whole-class modelling, then group writing.	103
Sequences	To recognize the acrostic form in poetry and understand its uses. To write poems in this style and polish them through redrafting.	Speaking and listening 1a, c; 2a, b; 3a, b. Reading 1a, c. Writing 1a, c; 2b. *As above.*	Writing poems in various sequential patterns.	Reading in four groups, whole-class discussion, then individual (or paired, or group) writing.	106
Shape poems	To use a sequential framework to write a poem. To identify and use alliteration.	Speaking and listening 1a, c; 2a, b; 3b. Reading 1a, c, d; 2a, b. Writing 1a, c; 2a, b. *As above.*	Experimenting with the techniques of writing shape poems, using alliteration and developing skills of presentation.	Whole-class reading and discussion, then individual writing.	108
Poetree	To compare different styles of shape poems (concrete poems and calligrams). To experiment with writing shape poems. To develop skills in written presentation of work. To learn some of the key terms used in writing poetry and understand what they mean.	Speaking and listening 1a, b; 2b; 3b. Reading 1a, c; 2c; 3. Writing 1a, c; 2b, e; 3b, c. *Knowledge about language, Level E.*	Using a published shape poem to help children learn about and understand a variety of terms used in talking about poetry.	Whole-class discussion, close reading in pairs, whole-class discussion, then paired writing.	111

Entries given in italics refer to the Scottish 5–14 Guidelines for English Language.

Listening and reading

Poetry is meant to be shared. The most direct way of sharing poems in the primary classroom is for you to read aloud to a group of children. If possible, arrange for the children to sit in comfort in a carpeted area where books are displayed. Encourage them to listen with interest and courtesy. When the poem is finished, suggest that the children think for a few moments before they start to talk. Explore the language used in the poems. It is useful to bring at least one new poem to each listening session, then let the children choose favourites to be re-read. They can anticipate what happens next, or be ready to join in the chorus. In this way, they build up an anthology of poems in their heads.

The teaching of poetry is integral to the teaching of reading. Many poems are fairly brief, and they can be a way of bringing children to books. Reluctant readers often appreciate the sound of the language used in rhyming and rhythmic poems. They get caught up in narrative poems, and enjoy the humour of funny poems. As well as reading quietly to themselves or out loud to each other, children can record poems onto cassette or use them as stimuli for artwork or drama.

An important characteristic of poetry books is that they don't have to be read through from cover to cover. Individual poems can be selected for reading at any one time, with no loss of involvement. A book is a readily portable item, and yet the reader can become 'lost' in it.

LISTENING FOR CLUES

To listen to a poem and discuss it. To be aware of how a poet's choice of words and phrases creates a particular impression.

†† *Class or group of 6–10.*

🕒 *20 minutes.*

Previous skills/knowledge needed

The children need to have had experience of listening to stories or poems read aloud in a group situation.

Key background information

The poem 'Nature Study' by Moira Andrew, which is used in this activity, contains two 'hidden clues': phrases which suggest what kind of day it was and the colour of the butterfly's wings. To recognize these clues, the children will need to listen with care. Other examples of 'hidden clue' poems suitable for reading aloud are 'City Bees' by Jennifer Curry, 'Foxy' by Matt Simpson and 'The Backs of Houses' by Rita Ray, which can all be found in *A Glass of Fresh Air* edited by Moira Andrew (Collins Educational, 1996).

Preparation

Familiarize yourself with the poem 'Nature Study' by Moira Andrew, so that you know where to find the 'hidden clues'.

Resources needed

The poem 'Nature Study' by Moira Andrew (see page 19); a range of poetry anthologies or collections; a full-colour illustrated guide to the identification of butterflies (such as *The Collins Gem Guide to Butterflies and Moths*); a board or flip chart.

What to do

Arrange the children in the most comfortable sitting position in the classroom, preferably in the library corner or similar carpeted area.

Tell the children that poets often hide clues within their poems, not always telling the whole story or revealing the picture behind the words. Discuss why they might do this, encouraging the children to suggest that readers and listeners should use their imaginations to get the most from a poem. Suggest that the children become 'poetry detectives', listening for clues hidden in poems. This means, of course, that they must listen carefully to the words and phrases in order to tease out the hidden details.

Read the poem 'Nature Study' aloud to the children. Initiate a discussion by asking easy questions to which all the children should have answers – for example: *What did the poet see? What time of day was it? What was the weather like?* Ask the children to remember the particular words, lines or images that gave them clues to the answers.

Repeat the lines: *'This butterfly / we couldn't identify'*. Explore with the children what these lines mean. How do you 'identify' a butterfly? What would help you to do this? Establish the need for an illustrated guide which shows, names and describes lots of different butterflies. Show the children the guide and leaf through it quickly.

Explore the image created in the words *'pitched / its bright tent'*. Ask the children to suggest other images for the way in which a butterfly opens its wings – for example, *'a beach umbrella put up in the rain'* or *'a flower opening its petals'*. Find ways of expressing these new images to fit into the pattern and style of the poem – for example, *'opened / its pretty petals...'*.

Discuss with the children the way in which the poet has suggested the pattern on the butterfly's wings. Ask them to recall the clues: *'studied symmetry'* and *'precise geometry'*. (Explain the use of the word 'studied' if necessary.) Why do they think the poet has used these mathematical descriptions – what does it say about the butterfly? Look again at the insect guide to check these ideas.

Go on to the clue which only really good listeners will pick up: *What colour was the butterfly?* Ask those who answer correctly to explain the clue that suggested that it was red: *'bloodied / the morning air...'*.

Suggest that 'Nature Study' is almost 'a photograph in words'. Read the poem again, asking the children to make a picture of the butterfly incident in their imagination. In particular, they should use visualisation to explore the effect of the last verse. *What is an 'after-image'? When might you see one?*

After you have finished reading and discussing the poem, allow a brief 'thinking space'. Ask for further questions or comments – for example, *Who might have been with the poet on this summer's day?* (She uses the words *'we'* and *'our'*, so we know that she wasn't alone.) Write out a verse of 'Nature Study' on the flip chart, and draw the children's attention to the 'butterfly' pattern of the lines: a single verb is the 'body' or hinge for the pair of 'wings'.

The children can finish off this listening session by talking about their own experiences of finding butterflies, dragonflies or moths. Encourage vivid description of the place, weather, colours and sounds.

Suggestion(s) for extension

Ask children to look through some of the poetry books in the classroom or school library. Can they find other poems which use a similar technique? Suggest that they explore one in detail. Encourage them to ask each other questions, building layers of understanding until they are able to 'paint a complete picture' in their imagination of the poem they have chosen.

Suggestion(s) for support

For children who have difficulty in following the poem, read through it again verse by verse, concentrating on simple questions whose answers can easily be teased out – for example, *What tells you it was a hot day?*

Opportunities for IT

Children could use an art package to create their own symmetrical butterfly pictures for display purposes. They could design one wing of their butterfly, perhaps using butterfly photographs to get ideas for patterns. Once they have completed the wing, they can make a copy of it; the copy can then be flipped over and positioned to meet the original wing.

Assessment opportunities

Note which children can listen effectively and offer thoughtful answers to your questions, showing that they understand the language of the poem and its implications.

Display ideas

Ask a group of children to draw individual butterflies in felt-tipped pen on art-quality paper, using the illustrated guide(s) as a reference and copying the patterns and colours with care. The drawings should be approximately life-sized. The butterflies can be cut out and attached to a frieze of summer flowers and grasses; the bodies only should be stuck down, so that the wings flap freely.

Nature Study

This butterfly
we couldn't identify
   pitched
its bright tent
on a roadside flower.

For a full minute
outstretched wings
   bloodied
the morning air
in studied symmetry.

Our eyes ached
with raw colour,
   remembered
pattern and shape
against eventual flight.

It drifted away
and precise geometry
   lingered
like an after-image
in the yellow heat.

Moira Andrew

I GOT RHYTHM, I GOT RAP

To consolidate listening skills. To develop a sense of rhythm and rhyme through clapping out and counting the syllables of a poem. To draft and write out a poem, then rehearse and perform it with percussion accompaniment.

†† *Whole class, then pairs or small groups (up to six).*

🕐 *40 minutes.*

Previous skills/knowledge needed

The children need to be able to look for rhyming words, and to clap out a regular rhythm. Most pop songs and any nursery rhyme could provide a background for this work. It will be helpful if the children have already done some preliminary work on syllables, perhaps starting with their own names.

Key background knowledge

This lighthearted activity introduces the theme of rhythm patterns. The children will need to understand that a rhythm is a regular pattern of stressed and unstressed syllables, and that many different rhythm patterns are possible in a poem. The activity also looks at rhyming words.

Preparation

Have ready a list of rhyming words for 'rap', such as *cap, trap, map* and so on. It may also be useful to practise reading Tony Mitton's poem 'Rebbit Rap' with a rap rhythm – which is not always easy the first time around! The whole of 'Rebbit Rap' appears in *Royal Rap* by Tony Mitton (Orchard Books, 1996); an extract is given on page 23.

Resources needed

Tony Mitton's poem 'Rebbit Rap' (see above); a copy of the traditional tale *The Princess and the Frog* (such as the version in *Grimm Tales*, retold and illustrated by Jan Ormerod, Walker Books 1990); writing materials; paste and brushes; a long roll of frieze paper (to back the completed poem); a board or flip chart; photocopiable pages 114 and 115 (see 'Suggestion(s) for support').

What to do

Ask the children whether they can explain what 'rap' is. Can they quote any rap lyrics? Bring out in the discussion that rap is a strongly rhythmic form that has been developed from Black African music.

Using a clapping rhythm to stress the beat, say the phrase: 'I got rhythm, I got rap!' Get the children to repeat the phrase, clapping out the beat. Count the syllables with them: **one**, two, **three**, four, **five**, six, **seven**. Now suggest that they find a second rhyming line which keeps to the rhythm, for example:

I got rhythm, I got rap,
I got a feather in my cap!

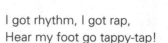

or

I got rhythm, I got rap,
Hear my foot go tappy-tap!

The children can work informally, in pairs or small groups, to come up with more second lines which keep to the rhythm and rhyme pattern. Make sure they realize that this activity is meant to be light-hearted, and that all you want is for everyone to think of a line.

Once you have exchanged new rapping rhythms, suggest that the children listen to the first part of Tony Mitton's rapping story. Read the opening verse of 'Rebbit Rap':

Back in the past
lived a little princess
with a real cute face
and a fancy dress.

Discuss how this opening sets the scene for the familiar tale of 'The Princess and the Frog'. Talk about the way in which the poem is written, noting its colloquial phrasing and strict rhyme. Repeat the verse together, clapping out the rhythm.

Go on to the second and third verses, leaving off the end-rhymes so that the children have to guess the missing words:

She was kinda fussy
(if you know what I mean)
'cos she knew that one day
she was gonna be a ... [queen].

Well, her family was rich.
(Her Daddy was King.)
So the princess had
'most ... [everything].

Look at the way the poet has used part-words: *'most, 'cos, gonna.* Discuss why these expressions have been used. Establish that keeping to the rhythm is vital in a poem of this kind, and that the language needs to be direct and 'punchy'.

Now work orally on the next part of the poem, missing out some lines (as shown below) and encouraging the children to fill the gaps. The children's suggestions may not be quite the same as the original; but that doesn't matter, as long as the essential rhythm and rhyme pattern is maintained.

Figure 1

Princess in a fancy dress

Her daddy was a King.

gold

She loved to play with her golden ball.

But of her toys
what she loved most of all
was ....
....
She carried it almost
everywhere
to ....
and ....
But one day she threw it
a bit too high.
The ....
in ....

Continue by reading the prose story of 'The Princess and the Frog', to tell (or remind) the children what happens next. Assist with 'skeletal storyboarding' (see Figure 1) on the board or flip chart to establish the sequence of events. Then suggest that the children work (in pairs or groups) on their own rap version of the fairy tale. Give out draft writing materials and allow the children a limited time, say ten minutes, to complete the task. Help out where children are stuck for a word or a line.

When the draft versions are complete, ask the groups to read some of their work aloud. At this point, you may need to help the children find ways to keep the strict rhythm going. Remember that the rules of rapping allow colloquial or part-words to make the lyric fit the beat, so that (for example) *y'all* is permissible in place of *you all* or *all of you*, and *'cos* can be used in place of *because*.

With the children's help, compile a sequence of the 'best bits' telling the whole story from beginning to end. Ask a member of each group to write out that group's contributions, then work with the other group representatives to paste the sections in place on a long backing strip, making a frieze.

To complete the activity, read the children's own version and Tony Mitton's complete 'Rebbit Rap' one after the other, encouraging the children to speak along with you. This will make for a noisy but thoroughly enjoyable session!

Suggestion(s) for extension

Suggest that more able children work in small groups, each group taking a different traditional tale (for example, 'Cinderella', 'The Princess and the Pea', 'The Three Billy-Goats Gruff' or 'The Little Red Hen') and following the above procedure to create their own rap version of the story.

Suggestion(s) for support

Help children who are having difficulty in retelling the story by sitting with a group and working with them. Using their ideas, make up a doggerel poem from another traditional story which they all know (such as 'Little Red Riding Hood'). Don't stick too closely to the original: make the session free-wheeling and as much fun as possible. Take the initiative by offering a verse and leaving off the last word or phrase – for example:

A silly little miss
in a red riding hood
went to visit Granny
way across ....

A big bad wolf
waited by a tree.
'I can see you
but you can't ....'

He ran to Granny's house
and jumped into bed.
'What great enormous teeth!'
the little girl ....

'Help' she shouted,
'Granny's on the floor!'
Then a hunky woodman
chased Wolfie ....

POETRY

Figure 2

chart. They could use paints or felt-tipped pens for the illustrations, writing out each verse of the poem alongside. The completed strip could be made up as a concertina book (see Figure 2).

Performance ideas

Raps are ideal vehicles for performance. While some children perform the rap, others could mime the events wearing simple costume items (crowns, a frog mask and so on). Adding percussion to the reading will help to enhance the effect of the rhythm on the audience. The children should maintain the rhythm steadily during the performance, and use a variety of voices for the narration. Such a performance will, of course, require careful rehearsal, with each child practising his or her contribution both individually and with the performing group.

Reference to photocopiable sheets

Photocopiable pages 114 and 115 can be photocopied onto thin card to provide cards for a game of 'Rhyming Snap' which will help children to recognize pairs of words which rhyme (see 'Suggestion(s) for support' above).

When they have completed a story like this successfully, encourage the children to work on their own rap poems. If necessary, help them with the first two lines of each verse.

Children who need help with finding rhymes can play 'Rhyming Snap', using photocopiable pages 114 and 115 copied onto sheets of card. They should cut out the two sets of cards, shuffle them together and try to identify the rhyming pairs.

Assessment opportunities

Note those children who pick up the rhythm of the rap with confidence, and try out various rhymes instead of sticking with the first idea that comes to mind. Also, note those who are confident enough to take risks by suggesting lines without having prepared the rhyming lines in advance. Look for children's readiness to share ideas, and their ability to communicate them clearly.

Opportunities for IT

Some pupils might like to draft and redraft their raps using a word processor. Alternatively, handwritten raps could be copied onto a word processor; the printed versions could be bound together to make a class book of raps. Children could add pictures to their rap poems, using clip art or their own line drawings scanned into a digital format. They could also explore ways of highlighting different words or syllables on the page to help the reader keep the rhythm going. This could be done by underlining, emboldening or using a larger font for stressed words or syllables.

Children could use a tape recorder to make a recording of their rap. They could also explore the use of a musical electronic keyboard to create a background beat and rhythm for their rap.

Display ideas

The children could illustrate the poem in a 'comic strip' format, following the storyboard sequence from the flip

Rebbit rap

Back in the past
lived a little princess
with a real cute face
and a fancy dress.

She was kinda fussy
(if you know what I mean)
'cos she knew that one day
she was gonna be a queen.

Well, her family was rich.
(Her Daddy was King.)
So the princess had
'most everything.

But out of her toys
what she loved most of all
was a tiny, shiny
golden ball.

She carried it almost
everywhere
to hold in her hand
and throw in the air.

But one day she threw it
a bit too high.
The ball flew up
in the big blue sky.

She held out her hand
but it fell beyond,
and it landed PLOP!
in the garden pond.

Well, the pond was dirty,
the pond was deep,
so the little princess
began to weep.

'Hey, now!' said a voice
from a bush close by.
'What's buggin' you?
Stay cool. Don't cry.'

Tony Mitton

This is part of 'Rebbit Rap' in *Royal Rap* (Orchard Books, 1996).

 RHYME TIME

To think about the sound of the words used in poems. To develop an understanding of rhyming words and rhyming patterns by reading and writing short poems that use rhyme.

✝✝ *Whole-class, group and individual work.*

🕐 *45 minutes.*

Previous skills/knowledge needed

The children should be used to listening to poetry with concentration and enjoyment. They should know that some poems rhyme and others don't. It will be useful if the children can remember some nursery rhymes from their early years' education; alternatively, and more probably, they can draw on their knowledge of television jingles and rhyming pop songs. It will also be useful if they know how to use a rhyming dictionary.

Key background information

This activity tackles one of the recurring problems in teaching poetry to children (or adults): they often insist that poems must rhyme – otherwise, they can't be called poems! This fact does indicate, however, that children are aware that *beat* (as in music) and *pattern* are important elements in poetry. Unfortunately, this vague understanding often leads to the production of doggerel – that is, clumsy verse in which the emphasis on rhyme and rhythm is to the detriment of language use and meaning. By actively promoting the use of rhyme, this activity tries to make children aware of when it is appropriate to use rhyme and when it would kill a poem stone dead!

Preparation

Before the activity, ensure that the children have access to a number of poetry anthologies and collections. Encourage them to assemble a class anthology of favourite poems (see Introduction, page 5). Make copies (one of each per child) of photocopiable pages 116 and 117.

Resources needed

Photocopiable pages 116 and 117; the children's choices in the class anthology, as suggested above; nursery rhyme books; a board or flip chart; writing materials and felt-tipped pens; rhyming dictionaries; a copy of *Does W Trouble You?* edited by Gerard Benson (Viking 1994).

What to do

Gather the children together as a class and show them a nursery rhyme collection. Ask whether anyone remembers the next lines after (for example) *Mary, Mary, quite contrary / How does your garden grow?* Make it a game, asking one child for the first line (or first two lines) of a well-known

nursery rhyme and choosing another child to finish it off. If they cannot remember the ending or get it wrong, ask children to make up new rhyming lines. This often leads to great hilarity; but make the point that rhyme helps us to remember a poem, and it can sound quite strange if new lines are invented.

Ask whether anyone can remember *There was an old woman / Who lived in a ...?* Try another version: *There was an old woman / Who lived up a tree/in a house/in a flat/ down a hole/in a box/under the sea ...* Divide the children into groups and give them five minutes to come up with a new version of the old rhyme, the only rule being that they must keep to the pattern and beat of the original. Bring the groups back together and share the new poems.

Give out copies of photocopiable pages 116 and 117. Read 'Nursery rhyme updated' with the children (see page 116). Discuss how the poet is using a nursery rhyme as the starting-point for a serious poem about homelessness, thus implying that our familiar and comfortable images of old people are in need of updating.

Reassemble the children in groups and make the task more difficult. For example, try *There was an old woman / Who lived in a bungalow/in a caravan/on a mountain/in a castle...*

There was an old woman
who lived in a bungalow.
She didn't like muddles,
wanted everything just so.

There was an old woman
who lived on a mountain.
They'd no running water,
so they bathed in a fountain.

... and so on. Give the children time to finish, perhaps with the help of rhyming dictionaries; then ask them to share their efforts with the others.

When the children are sitting together again as a class, ask a few of them to read out their favourite rhyming poems.

Discuss why they particularly liked each one. It is likely that most of the poems chosen will be humorous. If so, take this opportunity to talk about the idea that rhyme often helps to create a fun poem. Read the poems 'No Excuses' by Andrew Collett (page 116) and 'Habits of the Hippopotamus' by Arthur Guiterman (page 116) with the children to reinforce this point.

Andrew Collett's poem is a bit of fun straight from the classroom. Read it through again and encourage the children to look for the rhyming words. Scribe the rhymes on the board or flip chart: *in/bin, space/face, door/before, strange/change*. Encourage the children to find more rhyming words that could have been used – for example, *space/...face, race, mace, lace, place, ace...* Set the children the task of using the rhyming dictionary to find less common words, such as *surface/... disgrace, embrace, commonplace...* and so on. Add these new words to the flip chart. Do this with each rhyme in turn. As an oral game, ask the children to

make up new verses for Andrew Collett's poem using some of the new rhyming words.

Now look at Arthur Guiterman's poem 'Habits of the Hippopotamus' in similar detail. Children usually love this one, because the sounds are so appealing. Again, get them to find new rhyming words, such as:
▲ bustle/hippopotomuscle/hippopotorustle
▲ custard/hippopotomustard/hippopotobackward
▲ just/hippopotomust/hippopotocrust
▲ omnibuses/hippopotomusses/hippopotofusses
Note that one of the above words isn't a true rhyme but a near-rhyme or half-rhyme: *mustard/backward*. This is allowed sometimes.

Explain to the children that it is a good rule of thumb to use rhyme where the poem is intended to be 'fun', but to keep to non-rhyming rhythmic or patterned poems when they are working on descriptions of things.

Finish the activity by reading and exploring two poems about movement: 'Biking' by Judith Nicholls and 'Racing the wind' by Moira Andrew (on photocopiable page 117). Discuss the way in which each poem is constructed. Both have just two words in every line: *Fingers grip / toes curl; / head down, / wheels whirl* and *eyes staring / nostrils flaring*. However, 'Biking' has four-line verses, rhyming on every second line; whereas 'Racing the wind' has two-line verses, rhyming on every line. The children should also note the use of tabs to create a 'step' effect across the page in 'Racing the wind'.

Ask the children to work on poems which follow the pattern in either of the above poems. Since both have a feeling of movement, the children should try working on a theme such as 'Trains', 'Planes', 'Machines', 'Horse-racing', 'Surfing', 'Dancing', 'Skateboarding' or 'Ice-skating'. There are two rules: these poems must have only two words per line, and they must rhyme.

For example, a child's poem might look like this:

Fires roar,
   balloons soar.
      Up high,
         balloons fly.
      Air boat,
      balloons float.
   Journey's end,
balloons descend.

When the drafting stage is finished, the children can share their work with the class. The poems can then be written out in 'best' format.

Suggestion(s) for extension

More experienced writers might like to find and read a poem which uses an extended rhyming pattern. For an excellent selection of rhyming poems, the children should browse through Gerard Benson's *Does W Trouble You?*

Suggest that children find as many rhyming words as they can for one of the following: *play, found, make, tea, break* – or another word of their own choice.

Suggestion(s) for support

With children who need a lot of help, go back to the nursery rhymes and try changing the openings to generate new versions. Instead of 'Mary had a little lamb', they could try 'Horace had a little hen' or 'Annie had a little ant'. Instead of 'Humpty Dumpty sat on a wall', they might try to create a version such as the following:

Silly Lily sat on a pin,
Silly Lily made a great din.
All the dinner ladies
and all the canteen
Couldn't mop Lily's eyes
till her poor face was clean.

The children will enjoy creating these rhymes (the sillier the better!), and it will help them to recognize and use rhyming words. If they find working individually too difficult, an adult scribing for a group can help the group to create a book of *Modern Nursery Rhymes for Today's Children.*

Assessment opportunities

Note the children's skill in listening and responding to poems. Look for those who have a good ear for rhyme and can use it effectively.

Opportunities for IT

The children could use a word processor or desktop publishing package to make a class anthology of their poems.

A more challenging activity would be to make an electronic version of the children's poems using multi-media authoring software. This software allows children to mix text, pictures and sounds together into an electronic anthology. The children could each be given a page for their poem. They could present the poem in an interesting way, using different fonts or styles, or even shaping the poem. They could also add pictures; these could be taken from collections of clip art, drawn with an art package or scanned from their own line drawings. Finally, the children could record themselves reading their poems by using a microphone attached to the computer. By placing and linking the sound file to the page, the reader of the poem can also listen to it as well. This would make the book attractive to younger children.

The easiest way to start this type of work is for the teacher to set up a framework for the class anthology, creating a title page and then linking it to a page for each child or group. The title page can list all the contributors' names, so that when the reader clicks on a name he or she is taken to that child's page. Backwards and forwards buttons can be attached to each page, so that the reader can move through the book a page at a time. Using a home button will enable the reader to go back to the title page in one jump. Such a project will allow older children to display a range of IT skills, and give teachers an opportunity to assess their overall IT capability.

Display ideas

The children's new versions of nursery rhymes, suitably illustrated, can be displayed together with the traditional ones. A 'wall' of rhyming words could be displayed, with some of the poems created from these rhymes inserted as 'windows'. The children's rhymes and poems, either written out or word-processed (see above), can be bound into a large floor book.

Reference to photocopiable sheets

The five poems provided on photocopiable pages 116 and 117 should be read and discussed with the children. They are examples of poems which use rhyme to a particular effect: to make a serious point ('Nursery rhyme updated'), to make the reader laugh ('No Excuses', 'Habits of the Hippopotamus') or to create the impression of regular movement ('Racing the wind', 'Biking').

TRICKY RHYMES

To practise listening for and using words that rhyme in less obvious ways, including near-rhymes or half-rhymes.

†† *Whole class, then groups.*

🕐 *30 minutes.*

Previous skills/knowledge needed

The children should have experience reading and listening to rhyming poems where the rhymes are fairly obvious. Some experience of using a rhyming dictionary would be useful.

Key background information

Despite the fact that this activity is based on the use of rhyme, it is worth reminding the children that poems don't always have to rhyme: many good pieces of work have been ruined by children trying desperately to squeeze in an inappropriate word on the end of a line in order to achieve a rhyme. Look at some contrasting rhyming and non-rhyming poems together to underline the point.

This activity should be regarded as a game, and not taken too seriously. It relies on quick wits: the child suddenly 'hearing' the possibility of a good rhyme and working out a way to fit it into the poem.

Preparation

If necessary, familiarize yourself with the use of a rhyming dictionary. Make one copy per child of photocopiable page 118. Make sure that some anthologies or collections of poems, as well as rhyming dictionaries, are available for use.

Resources needed

Photocopiable page 118; a board or flip chart; anthologies and collections of poems; rhyming dictionaries; coloured pencils or felt-tipped pens, paper.

What to do

When the whole class is assembled, ask the children whether they can remember any rhyming poems or jingles – even odd lines which they can say aloud. Be prepared for anything, from 'Remember, remember, the fifth of November' to the latest television advert or an unsuitable limerick! Tell the children that many years ago, nursery rhymes were a way of telling illiterate people about serious events – for example, 'Ring-a-ring-a-roses' is thought to be about the havoc caused by the 'Black Death'. Ask whether they can work out what the following lines might mean:

A-tishoo, a-tishoo
We all fall down!

Discuss the simple rhyming words which make up most nursery rhymes – for example, *wall/fall* and *men/again* in 'Humpty Dumpty' and *Horner/corner*, *thumb/plum*, *pie/I* in 'Little Jack Horner'. Ask the children to find some simple rhymes for these words – for example, *wall/... ball, tall, small*. Now suggest that they try to think of some more difficult, sophisticated rhymes – for example, *stall, recall, enthrall, footfall* and so on. Make this a rapid-fire oral game, with one child suggesting a word and others trying to find as many rhymes for it as possible.

Give out copies of photocopiable page 118. Ask the children whether they can find a pair of 'difficult' rhyming words, such as *ocean* and *commotion*. Scribe a pair of words on the flip chart, and ask whether anyone can think of other rhymes to add to this pair – for example, *potion, promotion, lotion* and so on. If near-rhymes or half-rhymes are suggested, such as *portion* or *beacon*, give these a label and list them on one side.

Take the words *ocean, motion* and *commotion* and ask whether the children can find a theme which could link these words – for example, an island, a yacht race, seagulls, an albatross flying onto a ship... Take some of the children's suggestions and try to weave a poem around the ideas. Show the children how you may have to cross out words and phrases, and how you can use arrows to move ideas around the chart. Thus

Is there an island under (in) the sun
where (waves) ships sail across the ocean?

might become:

Paradise
Island in the sun,
restless blue ocean,
gulls free-wheeling,
causing a commotion.

Divide the class into groups. Ask them to use coloured pencils to circle the pairs of rhyming words on photocopiable page 118: one pair in red, another in blue, and so on. Now ask them to choose a pair from which to make up their own rhyming poem. Give them ten minutes to complete this task. Encourage them to use drafting techniques, and not to get bogged down by a concern to 'get it right first time'. Reassure them that you want them to try a variety of short poems, using different rhymes from the sheet. When they have finished, the groups can share their poems with the others.

Now discuss the idea of 'near-rhymes' or 'half-rhymes' with the children. Go back to the near-rhymes on the flip chart. Can the children find examples of near-rhymes on photocopiable page 118 (for example, *surface* and *palace*)? Ask them to suggest other near-rhymes – for example,

POETRY

glade/slide, home/alone, tune/balloon. Emphasize that such rhymes are often quite acceptable in a poem, and can sometimes add a 'magic' ingredient of surprise and mystery to an otherwise ordinary piece of writing.

Encourage the children to write more rhyming poems using the words on page 118 as starters, but adding to the list of rhymes (using full rhymes or near-rhymes, as they prefer). They can work in pairs or in a large group. Remind them that rhyming dictionaries are available.

When they have finished, seat the children together as a class and ask the groups to read out or perform the rhymes they have created. Those who are not reading should be encouraged to listen with interest and courtesy.

Suggestion(s) for extension

Suggest that more confident children look in the rhyming dictionary to make up more sets of 'difficult' rhyming words. They should choose a starting word and try to find about six rhymes for it, then write the rhymes on a piece of paper and pass it to the next person on the right. That child should then use the words as the basis of a new rhyming poem.

Suggest that the children make up rhyming poems from their own or other children's names – for example:

▲ *Look lively... it's Ivy!*
▲ *Hurry... it's Murray!*
▲ *Be quick... it's Nick!*
▲ *Climb the gate... it's Kate!*

(See David Horner's poem 'Reggie... take the register!' in *Read a Poem, Write a Poem* edited by Wes Magee, Blackwell,1989.)

Suggestion(s) for support

Encourage less confident children to make up new nursery rhymes, substituting different names and different animals – for example, 'Henry had a little cat' or 'Patsy had a little dog'. These rhymes can be as silly as the children wish, since zany ideas may well lend themselves to the unusual use of rhyme. The children's rhymes can be made into a new nursery rhyme book.

Assessment opportunities

Look for children who have a wide vocabulary, and can understand and use sophisticated words such as *commotion, promotion, locomotion* and so on. Listen for those whose ability to use rhyme is underdeveloped and in need of further practice.

Opportunities for IT

The children could write, edit and redraft their poems using a word processor. An alternative activity might be for the teacher to create (and save to a disk) a number of simple nursery rhyme lines, leaving gaps for the children to fill in as they wish. The children could then load these into the word processor and create their own lines:

Harry ...... sat on the ......
(Harry Hall sat on the wall)
Jack and ...... went up the .....
(Jack and Jane went up the lane)

A teacher working with older children could create a file with a complete rhyming poem and then ask the children, either individually or in small groups, to create a new poem by changing the rhymes and the accompanying text.

Display ideas

The children's own rhyming poems can be collected in floor books, each facing page being illustrated with paints or felt-tipped pens. Alternatively, the children could make up a floor-book anthology of 'unusual' rhyming poems with selections from books on the classroom shelves, or using poems which they have brought from home.

Performance ideas

The children who have written 'new' nursery rhymes might enjoy working together to prepare a recital of the 'old' and 'new' versions and then to present them in a class assembly.

Reference to photocopiable sheets

The list of words on photocopiable page 118 can be sorted into pairs or threes which rhyme. Some of the rhymes are full (conventional) rhymes; others are near-rhymes or half-rhymes. The sheet can be used as a stimulus for creative work involving the same or further rhymes.

THE HOUSE ON THE HILL

To develop the capacity for sustained listening. To explore, explain and share ideas on how a poem is constructed. To respond to a poem through imaginative role play and a class reading.

†† *Whole class, then four groups.*

🕐 *30 minutes.*

Previous skills/knowledge needed

The children should be used to listening to other children with attention and courtesy. They should be able to reason and speculate from the facts presented to them in the poem, exploring and exchanging their ideas.

Key background information

This activity is (probably) not based on the children's personal experience, and will therefore involve them in the active use of imagination and a certain amount of role-play. Make sure that the children understand that the poem used is a work of fiction, and that – although there is no need for them to be afraid – they will need to *imagine* how they would feel if they were to approach 'the House on the Hill'. This activity highlights the children's ability to listen carefully, absorb information and make an appropriate response.

Preparation

Prepare a cassette recording of Wes Magee's poem 'The House on the Hill' (see page 119), preferably read in a 'spooky' tone by an anonymous voice (which will not be recognized by the children). Make one A4 copy per child of photocopiable page 119, and an A3 copy for display.

Resources needed

Photocopiable page 119; a board or flip chart; a cassette recording of 'The House on the Hill'.

What to do

Tell the children that a dire warning has been received on tape. Say that you will discuss the contents with them after they have listened carefully to the message. Play the tape, but don't give any more clues until it is finished. The children won't know what to expect, and their reactions usually vary from earnest disbelief to laughter. By the end of the poem, most of them should be joining in the chorus.

Ask who might have visited the house on the hill and why. The children should consider whether the story is convincing or not. Encourage them to explain and justify their views – for example:

▲ It's not true that the piano would bite your fingers off, or blood would come out of the taps. Things like that don't happen.

▲ It could well be true that people who go to the house run away in panic, or that there are bones on the cellar steps. These things are possible.

Encourage them to discuss the case for and against the story's possible truth. Establish that the poem is a work of fiction, whether it 'could' be true or not.

Read out the first verse of the poem. Ask the children

29

to suggest how long ago the house was built, and what it looks like. Are there towers? Shutters? Steps leading up to the door? Suggest that the children try to imagine 'the madman who lived on the hill'. What was his name? What did he look like? What was his personality like? Read out the rest of the poem, encouraging the children to join in the chorus.

Through questioning and discussion, lead the children to explore the poem:

▲ Look at how it builds up suspense, using a combination of humour and menace.

▲ Ask the children to try and remember what booby-traps are scattered around the house. Discuss which one they consider to be the scariest, and why.

▲ Look at the ways in which the poet keeps the reader's interest throughout the poem.

▲ Discuss lines that amuse the children, such as 'then you're ice cubes... for sure.'

▲ Look at the way the rhyming pattern is kept going.

▲ Listen again to the last few lines and the way that Wes Magee has found to slow down the pace of the poem. What effect does this have?

▲ Ask the children: *If you were one of those children who is being warned not to go near the house on the hill, what would you do? Would you ignore the warning and climb the hill, or would you keep clear of the place? Why?* Discuss how different people respond to warnings.

Give out copies of photocopiable page 119 and ask the children to read the poem through silently. Put up an enlarged copy of page 119 on the wall. Now divide the class into four groups, and suggest that each group takes on a different role:

▲ One group can be the 'madman', creating more and more

booby-traps, going from room to room – the ballroom, hall, bedrooms, kitchen, cellar, attic and so on. Try to maintain a sense of fun, as the poet has done. There could be a servant-ghost waiting with a bucket of water above the door; a collapsing bed which swallows you up; a kitchen bin overflowing with nasty things. The group should draft out their ideas into a new verse, matching the style of the others and ending with the chorus. Tell them that they should be ready to read out the verse to the whole class later.

▲ Another group can be newspaper or TV reporters, trying to find out the truth about the spooky house. Appoint an editor who sends out a team of ace reporters. Suggest the questions that he or she would like answered – for example:

• *Where is the madman who lived on the hill hiding?*

• *What do the neighbours think of him?*

• *Can any of the neighbours describe this man?*

• *What sounds do they hear from the house at night?*

▲ The children in a third group can take on the roles of neighbours, and act out an interview with the journalists. Give everyone time to think of appropriate questions and responses. They will be asked to perform this interview at the end of the activity.

Another group can take on the roles of inquisitive children who ignore all the warnings and decide to explore the house on the hill. Suggest that everyone in this group contributes ideas towards a new verse. Encourage them to describe their terrifying experiences, saying what they heard, what they saw and how they felt – for example:

The door creaked as I opened it.
The house was dark as night inside.
I heard a bat squeaking, felt its wings
brush my face. I screamed. But –
nobody came. Then I heard footsteps...
If you go to the House on the Hill for a dare
remember my words...
                    'There are dangers. Beware!'

With the children's help, draft out the result. Ask a member of the group to read it aloud to the group, as a rehearsal for reading it aloud to the whole class.

As far as possible, 'The House on the Hill' should be an oral exercise. Points for each group to follow should be scribed on the flip chart as you go along. The groups should work separately. After ten minutes, bring the class back together and ask the groups to share their ideas. Keep the tone fairly light-hearted, with as much interesting discussion as possible. The children's new verses should be written in rough (though they could be copied out in 'best' later).

Finally, share a performance of the whole poem. Ask each group to read one verse, either with individual children reading lines or as a choral reading by the whole group. New verses can also be read out by the groups responsible for them.

scanned from a photograph (and maybe altered in an art package to make it spookier) or from their own line drawings.

Children could also use an art or drawing package to create a poster warning of the dangers of the house on the hill, or reinforcing the need to take care in other situations ('DON'T GO NEAR THE RIVER', 'DON'T PLAY WITH MATCHES', and so on).

Display ideas

The children could work on a silhouette outline of the house on the hill, making it look as spooky as possible – for example, a black cut-out on a dark blue background.

Performance ideas

The class could present 'The House on the Hill' as an entertainment for a school assembly or open evening. This could include:

▲ an atmospheric reading of the original poem;

▲ a drama with children in role as TV and newspaper reporters, 'the madman who lives on the hill', children who have been scared, neighbours, ghosts and so on;

▲ children who have written new poems or verses reading them out during the performance.

Reference to photocopiable sheet

The poem on photocopiable page 119 is the stimulus for the various parts of this activity. The photocopiable itself should be given to the children after they have listened to the poem, and before they embark on role-play and creative writing activities linked to the poem.

Suggestion(s) for extension

More able children could work on creating a similar 'spooky' poem in a different location – for example, 'The Monastery on the Mountainside', 'The Castle in the Caves', 'The Tunnel under the Town' or 'The Fortress in the Forest'.

Let the children brainstorm ideas for unlikely booby-traps to catch the unwary visitor. They could go on to describe these traps in a new version of the poem. They can write out each verse inside a hinged 'door' on a large picture of the haunted house.

Suggestion(s) for support

Children who find it difficult to express their ideas in front of the whole class could work in a small group with a supportive adult. The adult should scribe for each child, asking him or her to think of something scary which might be found in the house on the hill. The examples could rhyme – for example:

> In the house on the hill
> is a door that squeaks like a rat,
> a bird that flies like a bat,
> a dog that meows like a cat,
> a ghost that swings like an acrobat.
> If you visit the House on the Hill for a dare
> remember my words...
> 'There are dangers. Beware!'

Assessment opportunities

Listen for the children who respond to the poem in interesting and appropriate ways, can express themselves and are able to discuss their ideas with others. Note those who are willing to be persuaded to a different point of view. Look specifically for skills in role-play and performance.

Opportunities for IT

The four groups could present their finished work using a word processor or desktop publishing package. The newspaper group could create a front page about the house, possibly adding a suitable picture. The picture could be

FAMILY ALBUM

To listen with care to a poem in order to explore the use of descriptive and figurative language. To compare and contrast poems on similar themes. To use photographs and published poems as stimuli for writing descriptive poems.

†† *Whole class, then individual work.*

🕐 *40 minutes.*

Previous skills/knowledge needed

The children need to have the appropriate vocabulary to describe visual characteristics of people, and be able to visualise people clearly when they are not present.

Key background knowledge

This activity is based on the idea that everyone is different: that there are quirks of character, facial expressions, details of appearance, age differences and so on which give every person his or her own individuality and makes that person instantly recognizable.

Preparation

Bring in some photographs of your own family members. Ask each child to bring to school a photograph of a relative who is not in the immediate family group at home – for example, a grandparent, aunt or uncle. Be sensitive to any children who may lack such family members, or who may have left relatives behind under difficult circumstances.

Obtain copies of some poems about relatives – ideally 'Child with a Cause' by Moira Andrew, 'Grandpa' by Judith Nicholls and 'Aunt Flo' by John Cotton, all of which appear in *All in the Family* edited by John Foster (OUP, 1993). Make one copy per child of photocopiable page 120.

Resources needed

Photographs of your own family members; children's photographs of relatives (see above); some poems about relatives (see above); a board or flip chart; photocopiable page 120; writing materials.

What to do

Ask the children each to hold up a family photograph (see above). Ask them to tell the class something about the people in the pictures: who they are, where they live, what things they like to do.

Ask a group of children to put their photographs face down and then to describe the people in the pictures. They may say, for example: *It's my granny. She looks nice... This is Uncle Fred. He's really my mum's uncle... This is Grandpa Brown. He's got glasses on.* Establish that, while such descriptions are helpful, we may need more details to gain a clear mental 'picture' of each relative for ourselves. It

might be worth asking: *What makes my granny look nice? Is it her smile? Her eyes? Her mouth pursed like a ripe strawberry?* and so on.

Turn over the cards and see whether the children can match the photographs to the verbal descriptions given by other children. Discuss how easy or difficult it was to identify the correct photographs. Would they recognize these people if they walked into the classroom? Are there extra details in the photographs which might help in the descriptions? For example: *my grandfather is a thin man with hardly any hair; my auntie always wears fly-away scarves.*

Ask the children to listen to some of the ways in which poets describe their relatives – for example, Moira Andrew's description of her grandmother in 'Child with a Cause':

> My grandmother was chicken-plump.
> She wore long earrings, smelled of
> Pear's soap and lavender water.

Discuss this description with the children. Can they see a picture of the poet's grandmother in their heads? What words suggest that she wasn't very slim? (Think about how chickens look in the supermarket.) What else can they learn about her from this excerpt? Talk about what makes this word-picture different from simply saying: 'My granny is nice'.

Now read them Judith Nicholls' description of her grandfather in 'Grandpa':

> Grandpa ...
> knots his frayed hankie
> like a parachute
> to cover fraying hair.'

Encourage the children to develop this word-picture, building on what they have heard. Ask them what else they would like to find out about this grandfather.

Now read the following passage from John Cotton's poem 'Aunt Flo' to the children. Ask them what this description tells them about Aunt Flo:

> **Aunt Flo**
> Was like a dumpling on legs, with a face as gentle
> With colour and wrinkles as a stored pippin,
> Her flesh rich and as yeasty as fresh bread.

Discuss this passage in some detail, again concentrating on the images: *wrinkles like a stored pippin, like a dumpling on legs, flesh yeasty as fresh bread.* Emphasize how these unusual images help readers or listeners to 'see' Aunt Flo in their heads. Suggest that the children practise using similar skills to build up a word-portrait of a relative, using a photograph.

Give each child a copy of photocopiable page 120. Ask the children to look quietly at the picture, trying to gather as much information from it as they can. Suggest that they give the picture a suitable title (such as 'Grandma', 'Great-Aunt Maisie' or 'Mrs Cuthbertson next door'). Write the most appropriate title on the board or flip chart.

Now discuss the face in the picture. How can the children describe her appearance? Wrinkled like an apple? As powdery as a fresh snowball? As twinkly as a star? What about the hair: fuzzy, fraying, curly; as grey as smoke? Using the children's suggestions, build up a word picture on the board or flip chart.

Now encourage the children to think what this woman might be like. Since they have never met her, they must use imagination to fill in the bare outline. What do they think she might wear? Is she fat or thin, or somewhere in between? What might she like to do, or to eat? Does she wear perfume, cologne, lavender water?

Build up the children's suggestions on the flip chart into a class poem. It might look something like the example shown below. Read over the class poem and correct any mistakes. Ask the children to copy it out. They can make changes to it if they wish.

Now settle the children down to listen to the three poems 'Child with a Cause', 'Grandpa' and 'Aunt Flo' (or three similar poems from another source). Discuss what they find out about each character. Point out that these are all 'memory' poems. Do the children think the old people in these poems are actual relatives of the poets? Why?

Use questions to compare and contrast the three poems in various ways – for example:
▲ What is unusual about the opening line of 'Grandpa'? How about the opening line of 'Aunt Flo'?
▲ Which of these three poems is a story? Why are the other two not really stories?
▲ How are the patterns these poems make on the page different?

Ask the children to look for phrases in each poem which would help them to draw a portrait of a character. Scribe some of these on the flip chart – for example, *My grandmother was chicken-plump* (from 'Child with a Cause'). What does this suggest about her appearance?

Go on to discuss the language of each poem in some detail – for example, looking at 'Child with a Cause':
▲ What does the phrase 'Grandfather kept us both on a tight rein' mean?
▲ Why do you think the child pushed her plate away? How do you think she was feeling?

Quote an example of alliteration in 'Aunt Flo'. Read the poem out again, asking the children to listen for more examples. *What effect does the alliteration have? What does the poet think about his aunt?*

With these poems in mind, encourage the children to draft out fuller versions of their word portraits of relatives. Whereas the previous versions were based only on the photographs, these poems should incorporate details of each person's life and personality (including their way of speaking).

Suggestion(s) for extension
Some children could complete their draft poems, read them to the class and write them out with appropriate illustrations. Children who are interested could find and read more poems in the anthology *All in the family*.

Suggestion(s) for support
Read out the short descriptive extracts above, one at a time. Help those who find listening difficult by going over each extract line by line, talking

Great-Aunt Polly

She is roly-poly,
round as a jam doughnut.
Behind wire glasses,
her eyes are shiny
as wet pebbles.
Her mouth is small,
painted red, pursed
like a ripe raspberry.
She likes to watch
Eastenders, reads
the Western Mail,
puts on a squashy hat
and goes to church
every Sunday, sucks
mints-with-a-hole.

through the language and content of each portrait – for example, *Have you ever seen old men wearing hankies on their heads? Why do they do this? Where can you see them? What makes Grandpa's hankie look like a parachute? What words tell you that Grandpa is growing old?* and so on.

Assessment opportunities

Note the children's ability to pick up separate pieces of information about the characters in the poems, and their skill in adapting these descriptive techniques into their own pieces of writing.

Opportunities for IT

The children could create a class album of their family poems. Some children might prefer to originate a poem using a word processor; others might use it to present their final draft. To make the album more interesting, children could use a scanned image of their family photograph to illustrate their work. They could add the picture to the page with their poem, and then format the page – perhaps allowing their poem to flow around the picture. Discuss with the children which layout will be most effective. The children could change the sizes of the picture and the fonts to make sure that their work fills the page.

The children might like to make a copy of their page to send to a relative. This could be sent along with a word-processed letter, explaining how they wrote their poem – and perhaps expressing hope that the relative enjoyed it.

Display ideas

The children could use their word portraits to make a 'gallery', sketching full-page pictures in very faint coloured pencil over each poem (or writing the poem on tracing paper and placing it over a strong outline sketch). Each of these combined portraits can be placed inside a thin card frame. (See Figure 3.)

Performance ideas

The children can dress up as the relatives about whom they have written poems, and read out these poems to an audience. This could be developed into a role-play session.

Reference to photocopiable sheet

Photocopiable page 120 shows a 'character' face which the children should use as a stimulus for descriptive and imaginative poetic language, resulting in a class poem about the character.

Figure 3

A face from a family album

PORTRAITS OF SUMMER

To develop the ability to listen with care to a poem and evaluate it, going on to compare and contrast poems on a similar theme and respond to them through discussion. To identify clues which suggest that a poem was written in a previous generation.

†† *Whole class.*

🕐 *30 minutes.*

Previous skills/knowledge needed

The children should have experience of listening to stories and poems being read aloud. They should be familiar with the conventions of listening and responding as a class, such as listening with courtesy and taking time to think about what they have heard before speaking. They should be ready to take turns to answer or make comments, and be used to sharing their thoughts and opinions.

Key background information

The poets whose work features in this activity were both born in the nineteenth century. Henry Wadsworth Longfellow (1807–82) was an American who worked for a time in Europe. Edward Thomas (1878–1917) was an Englishman who served in the First World War and wrote much of his poetry during this time. The two poems reproduced on photocopiable page 121 both evoke a powerful sense of summer. Although they were written many years ago, they have quite a contemporary feel. It is important for the children to be aware that people who lived in times past experienced many of the same sensations as we do: the sound of rain or birdsong has not changed in a hundred years – or a thousand!

Preparation

Obtain a reference book on wild flowers, such as the Collins Gem Guide *Wild Flowers* by Marjorie Blamey and Richard Fitter (Collins, 1980); some photographs of old-time railway trains, stations and signals; and some pictures on a 'summertime' theme. Make sure that anthologies and collections of poetry are available in the classroom. Make one copy per child of photocopiable page 121.

Resources needed

Photocopiable page 121; 'summertime' pictures; old-time railway photographs; a reference book on wild flowers; paints and paper; anthologies and collections of poetry (see 'Suggestion(s) for extension').

What to do

Arrange for the children to sit comfortably, preferably when there are likely to be no interruptions, so that they can concentrate on listening. Tell them that you have two poems about summer and you want them to listen carefully to both, making pictures of the scenes inside their heads. Remind the children that you will leave a 'thinking time' after each poem and that they should be quiet during that time; and that later, you will ask some questions about the poems.

Read out 'Adlestrop', followed by 'Rain in Summer' (see page 121). Give the children a 'thinking time' of about two minutes. Then ask them to talk about the pictures that they have made in their heads through listening to the poems. Ask about seasons, weather, places. What differences do they notice? Contrast one poem with the other. What kind of day was it in each poem? They are both about summer, but are describing different kinds of weather, atmosphere and mood. Look at the photographs and pictures together,

asking the children to comment on the differences between what is shown and what they would see now.

Give out copies of photocopiable sheet 121. Ask the children to consider the sounds referred to in these poems: in 'Adlestrop', the hiss of steam from the train, someone clearing his throat, birds singing; in 'Rain in Summer', the sounds of the rain hitting the roofs and pouring down the overflow spout and the gutter. Talk about how the sound descriptions help to bring the poems alive. Are there other sounds the children would like to add to these poems? Why?

Talk about the colours in the poems. Which is the dominant colour in the Thomas poem: yellow, orange, green? What about the Longfellow poem: grey, blue, brown? Can the children find evidence in the words to support their impressions of colour?

Think about why Longfellow welcomes the rain in his poem. Talk about hot days when your clothes stick to your back, when the air is so close that you can hardly breathe. Discuss why it is important not to get too much sun: sunburn, headaches and so on. Talk about what the children can do to prevent being burned by the sun: wearing hats and T-shirts, putting on sun creams, sitting in the shade and so on.

As a digression, explore the children's experiences of sunshine – when it is just what they have longed for all winter; how it feels on bare arms; how suitable it is for picnics and holidays. Ask them to think about what they see when sunshine parches the grass and flowers, when it makes colours in windows, when it brings daisies out like a rash on the grass (after rain).

Read through 'Rain in Summer' again. Remind the children of the dates when H.W. Longfellow was alive; then encourage them to think about his experience of 'the welcome rain'. Prompt them to consider how the words that he wrote down can still make us feel the dust and heat of a long-ago summer, help us to hear the sound of rain as *it gushes and struggles out / From the throat of the overflowing spout!* Discuss other ways in which people who have died can still share something of their lives with us: through stories, paintings, photographs, records and so on. Do some words and phrases used by these two poets give clues that the poems were written a long time ago?

Read through 'Adlestrop' again. Explore this poem in more detail. Where was Edward Thomas? Why was nobody around at the station? Where was the steam which 'hissed' coming from? Use a suitable reference book to find pictures of the wild flowers he mentions. Encourage the children to think about how the poet uses words and images to bring his unexpected stop at Adlestrop right into the classroom. *And for that minute a blackbird sang / Close by...* What does this line tell us? Elicit comments such as: *Nothing else was making a sound. Everything was still and peaceful.* Use the photographs and pictures to give some historical background. Can the children see why this quiet rural scene might have meant so much to the poet at that time?

Before you complete this listening and reading session, ask the children to think over the sights and sounds that these two poets have brought into their imagination. Suggest that they follow up the activity by painting the scene described in one of the poems.

Suggestion(s) for extension

More able children could look through poetry anthologies and collections for more poems about summer. Suggest that they choose one or more that particularly appeals and copy it out in 'best' writing or on the word processor. Make up a group anthology of summer poems, perhaps with illustrations.

Suggestion(s) for support
Less confident children may need a support teacher to work directly with a group, guiding them with fairly straightforward questions about the poems – for example: *What month of the year was it when the train stopped at Adlestrop station? What kind of bird did the poet hear singing? Look at 'Rain in Summer' – which words tell you how the rain was falling?*

Assessment opportunities
Note the children whose listening and reading skills are well-developed. Look for those who can deduce from the poems things that are not made explicit. Look out for children who find it difficult to sit still and concentrate throughout such a listening session.

Opportunities for IT
Children could present their summer poems using a word processor, perhaps adding their own graphics to represent summer. They could even scan their own summer drawing onto the page and use it as a background for their writing. They could also use a tape recorder to record summer sounds (waves, gulls, a cricket match, a lawnmower and so on), which could be played when the children are reading and performing poems about summer.

These sounds could be added to a multi-media presentation of the summer poems, possibly adding summer music recorded from a CD-ROM ('Summer' from Vivaldi's *Four Seasons* or Mendelssohn's *Midsummer Night's Dream Overture*) or composed by the children as a background to the poems.

Display ideas
Copies of poems about summer which the children have chosen could be attached with paste to a summer frieze, with sunshine on one half and rain on the other.

Performance ideas
Wearing clothes appropriate to the poems (sunhats and sunglasses for the sunny day; peaked caps, raincoats and boots for the rainy day), the children can read aloud poems about summer which they have chosen to include in a class anthology. A 'sounds of summer' cassette could be prepared (for example, with the sounds of waves, gulls, an ice-cream van, a summer storm and so on) and played to accompany the reading.

Reference to photocopiable sheet
Photocopiable page 121 contains two poems which should be read out to the children, discussed and then given to them for reading and further discussion.

Portraits of summer

Adlestrop

Yes, I remember Adlestrop –
The name, because one afternoon
Of heat the express-train drew up there
Unwontedly. It was late June.

The steam hissed. Someone cleared his throat.
No one left and no one came
On the bare platform. What I saw
Was Adlestrop – only the name

And willows, willow-herb, and grass,
And meadow sweet, and haycocks dry,
No whit less still and lonely fair
Than the high cloudlets in the sky.

And for that minute a blackbird sang
Close by, and round him, mistier,
Farther and farther, all the birds
Of Oxfordshire and Gloucestershire.

Edward Thomas

from **Rain in summer**

How beautiful is the rain!
After the dust and heat,
In the broad and fiery street,
In the narrow lane,
How beautiful is the rain!

How it clatters along the roofs,
Like the tramp of hoofs!
How it gushes and struggles out
From the throat of the overflowing spout!

Across the window-pane
It pours and pours;
And swift and wide,
Like a river down the gutter roars
The rain, the welcome rain!

H.W. Longfellow

TELL ME A STORY

To experience poetry as narrative through listening to, reading and discussing a range of narrative poems.

†† *Whole class, three groups.*

🕐 *45 minutes.*

Previous skills/knowledge needed

The children should be used to listening to stories and poems, and should be confident in expressing their ideas and opinions about what they have heard. They should have some experience of predicting what might happen next in the course of a story.

Key background information

This activity relies on three skills: listening, prediction and discussion. Encourage the children to exchange ideas and opinions on the content of the poems which they have heard or have read for themselves. In some cases, the children will be required to identify with the poet and imagine the circumstances in which a poem was written.

Preparation

Ask each child to borrow a favourite story book from home, or to choose one from the school library. They should be able to précis the story and say what made it special for them. Find a copy of 'The Rime of the Ancient Mariner' by Samuel Taylor Coleridge (the Classic Words & Image edition of 1992 is particularly well illustrated). Make one copy per child of photocopiable pages 123, 124 and 125, and some copies of photocopiable page 122 (for teacher use, also see 'Suggestion(s) for support'). Make sure that anthologies or collections of poetry are available in the classroom.

Resources needed

Poetry anthologies and collections; photocopiable pages 122 to 125; children's favourite stories (see above); a board or flip chart.

What to do

Initiate a discussion about stories, exploring all the different ways that we can enjoy a story – by reading, writing or listening to it, or by watching a performance of it. Discuss the storylines in television 'soap operas'. Can the children explain what it is that gets them 'hooked on' such programmes? Is it something about the situation, the characters, their adventures? Do the children feel curious about where the characters live, what they do, how they feel? When they are talking about the feelings of characters, ask the children to consider why we care about characters in books and on television. Take time to explore this aspect of the discussion.

Still working with the whole class, read 'The *Alice Jean*' (photocopiable page 122) aloud. Allow a minute's thinking time, then get a discussion going to show how such a poem can be explored in depth. What was the *Alice Jean*? Where were the people? Why had they gathered there? What do you think had happened? What did the old woman think had happened? Use the board or flip chart to note the essentials of the story.

Now read the third verse again:

> Then one old woman stared aghast:
> 'The 'Alice Jean'? But no!
> The ship that took my Ned from me
> Sixty years ago –
> Drifted back from the utmost west
> With the ocean's flow?

Encourage the children to express how the old woman must have felt. Ask whether they think she was right. What did she believe about the ocean beyond the horizon? What did some of her friends and neighbours think? How can the children tell this? (*A hundred women gaped at her, / The menfolk nudged and laughed...*) Talk about how the old woman felt when the others ganged up against her and laughed at her. Have any of the children ever been in a similar situation? (If a child talks about bullying, listen with care, but do not expand on the theme at this time.)

Ask the children to think about the ending. Do we really know what happened to the *Alice Jean*? The children should be aware that this 'ghostly ship' may be a ghost, not a 'real' ship. Encourage them to consider what might happen next – or later.

Ask the children about the sound of the words in this story. Which are the rhyming words in each verse? Discuss the idea of a 'narrative poem': what are the advantages of telling a story in this form? Show the children the shape

the words make on the page. Ask the children whether they can remember some of the descriptions which helped them to make a picture in their heads – for example, *waters black as ink*, *foaming seas*.

Divide the children into three groups. Give out copies of the poems 'Miller's End', 'The Apple-raid' and 'Act of Worship' (photocopiable pages 123 to 125), each group concentrating on a different poem. Tell the children that they have ten minutes to read and discuss the poem. Direct them to think about what story is being told in the poem, how the people were feeling and why the poem was written. They should try to tease out as much meaning as they can from what they are reading.

When the ten minutes are up, bring the class together. Ask each group to tell the others as much as they can remember of the poems they have read. They should use the earlier discussion of 'The *Alice Jean*' as a guide for their comments.

Now read all three poems aloud, one after the other, so that everyone can share them. Encourage the children to ask more questions, and to suggest other ways in which each poem might have ended – or predict what happened next. What words or phrases helped them to imagine the scenes described in the poems?

Ask the children to think about what happened to John Peters in 'The Apple-raid'. Was there another possible ending to this poem? How do they think the poet might have been feeling when he wrote the poem? Do they think it is a true story?

Look at the lines: *...We stored the fruit / In pockets and jerseys until all three / Boys were heavy with tasty loot* and *I wonder if David remembers at all / That little adventure, the apples' fresh scent?* Explore with the children the way that these lines paint a picture of a long-ago adventure, especially in their use of sense words. Remind the children how they can sometimes make their own writing come alive by 'thinking through the senses'.

Now look at 'Act of Worship', another memory poem. Can the children form a mental picture of the grandfather and grandmother from the descriptions in the first and second verses? What were they wearing? From what the poem says later, why should Grandmother have *won a medal for bravery*? What was she afraid of? What does the phrase *No head for heights* mean? Can the children think of other things that people do where a 'head for heights' is essential? (For example, being a pilot, a mountaineer or a window-cleaner.)

Ask the children: *Why would Grandmother not say she was frightened in the upstairs front pew of the church. Why did she always pass round the peppermints? How can you tell that this poem is written about something that happened a few decades ago?* (The 'fur tippet', the 'gold watch chain' and even the 'paper bag' for the peppermints are all details which place this story in the past.) *Which line suggests that Grandfather might have gone to church more to be seen than to worship?*

Turn now to 'Miller's End'. What kind of story do the children think this is: a mystery, a ghost story, a memory?

How do they feel about it? What does the ending tell us? Can the children suggest what might have happened in the garden?

Finish off the session by reinforcing the idea that a poem can tell a story. In the old days, *ballads* were a popular way of telling stories. These were passed on from one story-teller to another, and they almost always used rhyme and rhythm to make them easier to remember. Suggest that the children try to find examples of the ballad form in poetry anthologies and collections. For example, they might find 'The Wife of Usher's Well' by Anon., 'The Charge of the Light Brigade' by Alfred, Lord Tennyson and 'The Pied Piper of Hamelin' by Robert Browning.

Suggestion(s) for extension

More able children might try writing a narrative poem based on a story in a local newspaper. Suggest that they keep it short, using either up to 100 words or up to five four-line verses. They could write out the completed poem inside a zigzag book, with illustrations.

Suggestion(s) for support

Instead of looking at one of the other photocopied poems in a group, less confident children could work with peer support to go over the story of 'The Alice Jean', already worked through by the teacher. They should be given copies of photocopiable page 122 for this, and should use the notes on the board or flip chart as a guide.

Assessment opportunities

Note the children who can read, listen to and discuss the poems with confidence. Look for those who can suggest alternative endings for the poems.

Display ideas

The children could draw characters from these poems on black paper to make silhouettes for a wall display of illustrated story poems.

Performance ideas

The children could tell the stories behind these narrative poems through role-play, using a few basic props such as Grandma's long earrings ('Child with a Cause'), Miss Wickerby's veil ('Miller's End') and some fresh apples ('The Apple-raid').

Reference to photocopiable sheets

Photocopiable pages 123, 124 and 125 feature three narrative poems which the children should read and discuss, thinking about both the content and the language used in each poem. Photocopiable page 122 can be given to less confident children, allowing them to go over a poem which has already been worked through by the teacher (see 'Suggestion(s) for support').

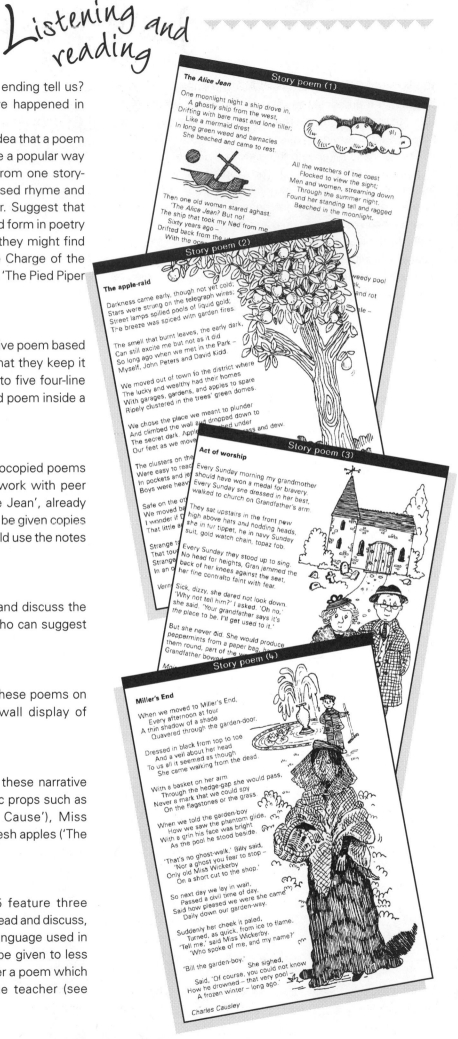

OLD JACK RAGS

To listen to a poem being read aloud and to analyse how the poem conveys a message, feelings and attitudes. To discuss their opinions on the poem's content.

†† *Whole class, groups, individuals.*

🕐 *30 minutes.*

Previous skills/knowledge needed

The children should be ready to listen with attention and courtesy. They should be able to share their ideas with others and respond sensitively to the content of the poem. They should have some awareness of the idea of prejudice and the realities of homelessness, and be able to empathize with someone living a very different life from their own.

Key background information

This activity is intended to stimulate children's thoughts about a poem they have listened to, and to encourage them to extend the poem by imagining what might happen next. The children will need to explore possible rhymes when extending the poem.

Preparation

Make one copy per child of photocopiable page 126.

Resources needed

Photocopiable page 126; a board or flip chart; writing materials.

What to do

Arrange for the children to sit together comfortably, ready to listen. Tell them that you have a poem to read and that they should listen quietly, without commenting, until you have finished. Read 'Sunlight or surprise?' (see page 126) aloud. Leave a short 'thinking time' before asking questions.

Ask how the poem made them feel. Collect a range of replies: 'sad', 'sorry for Jack Rags', 'concerned' and so on. Scribe some of the responses on the board or flip chart. Explore some of the reasons for homelessness. Discuss the fact that the children may have seen homeless people begging, sleeping in doorways or selling *The Big Issue*. Take time to talk through the children's experiences and observations. Read out the poem again, suggesting that they join in the chorus line.

Give out copies of photocopiable page 126 and ask the children to read it through in silence. Why do they think the child in the poem has been told not to go near Old Jack Rags? Are any of these reasons valid? Might some of the things that 'people say' about him possibly be untrue? Is there anything they say which is definitely not true? Make this an open discussion, encouraging and accepting all kinds

of comments. Scribe some of these observations on the flip chart (for the writing task later).

Encourage the children to think about some of the harsh comments made by 'people': *Don't go near him... He's full of fleas* and *He lives on rubbish, sleeps in dirt*. Do they think the people who made these comments have got to know Jack Rags, or ever stopped to talk with him? Encourage the children to contrast these attitudes with the innocence of the child who asks direct questions: *'Do you sleep in dirt?... And eat small children?'*

Ask the children to suggest questions that they would like to have asked the old man. Encourage them to think of questions such as: *What happened to your home? Did you ever have a place of your own? Do you have a family? Where are they now?*

Divide the class into groups. Ask the children whether they can predict what happened next. Did Old Jack Rags move on? Did he find a place to live? Did he unexpectedly meet a long-lost son or daughter? Ask each group to put together notes for a follow-up scenario. Make sure that the children have noticed and talked about the last verse:

> Then was it sunlight or surprise
> That made those tears start from the eyes
> Of Old Jack Rags?

Ask the children to consider what it was that made Old Jack sad enough to cry. Suggest that they look at the poem's title. Can they think of a different title – or one which, in their opinion, is better?

When the groups have made some notes on what might have happened next, suggest that they compose some follow-up verses – perhaps using the pattern of the poem as a guide. They should refer to the set of comments recorded earlier on the flip chart. For example, a group might come up with:

> 'Have you got a son?' I asked,
> 'Or anyone special from your past,
> Poor Old Jack Rags?'

> 'All my family's long been dead.
> There's nobody else – just me,' he said,
> Sad Old Jack Rags.

Other children (again working from some of the comments on the flip chart) might prefer to write about their responses to the poem. This might take the form of an objective report on 'the facts', a piece of expressive prose or a poem using quite a different pattern from 'Sunlight or surprise?'. The children should be given an open choice of response, as long as their work is relevant to the poem.

Suggestion(s) for extension

More able writers could make up a poem about a conversation with Old Jack Rags. If they decide to follow the pattern of the original poem, they could start with other people's comments about the old man – for example:

> 'Don't go near that awful old tramp
> Sitting outside in the cold and damp,
> That Old Jack Rags.'

> 'OK Dad, I'll pretend he's not there,
> But I don't think we're being very fair
> To Old Jack Rags...'

If they choose to write in a different style, remind the children to try and bring out some of the simplicity and sadness of the original piece.

As a follow-up task, ask the children to write a prose description of the scene in up to 100 words.

Suggestion(s) for support

Ask an adult helper to read the poem again to children who have found it difficult to understand and appreciate. Through discussion, help them to think about the feelings of the tramp: his loneliness, his lack of comfort and so on. To strengthen their understanding of what the poem is about, ask the children to change one or two words in each verse, but to keep the sense – for example:

> No, don't go near him, mothers say,
> He's full of nits, so keep away
> From Old Jack Rags.

> He's never washed, he's never clean,
> The dirtiest tramp you've ever seen,
> Is Old Jack Rags.

Assessment opportunities

Note the children who are able to recognize and appreciate what the poem is saying. In particular, look for immediate awareness that some of the things 'people say' are unreliable: though the tramp is none too clean, 'He eats small children with his bread' is a fairly wild claim. They may recognize what brings adults to lie and exaggerate in this way. Note the children who empathize with the old man, and who hear what the poet is really trying to say in the last verse: *Then was it sunlight or surprise / That made those tears start from the eyes / Of Old Jack Rags?*

Opportunities for IT

More able pupils could write their précis using a word processor. They should be shown how to use the word count facility to make sure that they do not exceed the word limit.

This activity is also an ideal opportunity for children to read a poem onto cassette, each child in the class or group reading one line and everyone joining in the chorus.

Figure 4

A poem for discussion

Sunlight or surprise?

No, don't go near him, people say,
He's full of fleas, so keep away
From Old Jack Rags.

He's never tidy, never clean,
The filthiest tramp you've ever seen,
Is Old Jack Rags.

He lives on rubbish, sleeps in dirt,
He's only got one grubby shirt,
Has Old Jack Rags.

His teeth are black, his eyes are red,
He eats small children with his bread,
Does Old Jack Rags.

No, don't go near him, people say,
But I went near, just yesterday,
To Old Jack Rags.

And: 'Do you sleep in dirt?' I said,
'And eat small children with your bread?
Well, Old Jack Rags?'

Then was it sunlight or surprise
That made those tears start from the eyes
Of Old Jack Rags?

Richard Edwards

Display ideas

The children could work together to paint a street scene with Old Jack Rags sitting on a wall, surrounded by rubbish, and a child (or several children) staring at him. This picture could include collage elements. It could be framed by examples of the children's writing, mounted on food wrappers (crisp packets, biscuit wrappers and so on) or scraps of torn newspaper. (See Figure 4.)

Performance ideas

This activity lends itself well to role-play. The poem could be performed with choral speaking, or used as the basis of an interview with Old Jack Rags for a local newspaper or TV station.

Reference to photocopiable sheet

The poem on photocopiable page 126 should be read to the children and then given to them for reading and discussion, leading to a choice of possible creative writing activities.

POETRY

ONE-PARENT FAMILY

To look at how a character is presented in a poem. To develop personal responses to the poem through discussion of the issues and attitudes which the poem addresses.

†† *Whole class, groups.*

⏱ *30 minutes.*

Previous skills/knowledge needed

The children should be used to listening with attention and courtesy, and to sharing their ideas with others in the group. They should have a wide vocabulary of words related to character and behaviour, and be able to use it in discussion.

Key background information

Although it is based on a specific poem, this activity can be used with many other narrative or descriptive poems. It encourages children to explore their feelings about parents, and to challenge popular expectations about the traditional roles of women and men. Although the poem deals with some possible difficulties of a 'one-parent family' in a fairly lighthearted way, you will need to be aware of any similar problems among the children in your class, especially if these have arisen recently.

In *Excuses, Excuses* (OUP, 1997), John Foster has collected poems about people you might meet in school; in *All In the Family* (OUP, 1993), he has collected poems about parents, grandmas, grandads, uncles, aunts, brothers, sisters and so on. You will find both of these anthologies really useful sources of 'character poems' for this and similar activities.

Preparation

Collect some books and poems about families (see above). Ask the children to lend you some family photographs; if possible, bring in a few of your own. Make one copy per child of photocopiable page 127.

Resources needed

Family photographs (see above); a board or flip chart; photocopiable page 127; writing materials; books and poems about families (see Suggestion(s) for extension').

What to do

Working with the whole class together, discuss some of the children's family photographs: themselves as babies, their brothers and sisters, their grandparents, holidays and so on. Encourage them to talk about the relationships between the people in the pictures. Don't press for too much detail: look for caption-style comments such as 'This is my grandma' or 'Here is my brother being a pain – as usual!'

Tell the children that you are going to read a poem called 'One-parent family', and ask them what they think will be in a poem with this title. Talk through their expectations: a mum on her own, a dad on his own, not having a lot of money and so on.

Set up a question and discussion session. Organize the children into groups and give them ten minutes to think about some questions – for example:

▲ *Who do you think will be in a family?*

▲ *Are grandmas, grandads, uncles, aunts, cousins and so on part of the family? If not, who is?*

▲ *What should dads do about the house?*

▲ *How do you think children ought to help at home?*

▲ *How can people keep in touch with members of the family who live a long way away?*

Discuss the children's answers and opinions with the whole class. Now pose the question: *What do you think a mother ought to be doing?* Use the board or flip chart to list some possible maternal qualities and tasks. Ask the children, working in groups, to rank them in order of importance, adding more as they think of them. For example:

Qualities	Tasks
kindness	cooking, baking
gentleness	DIY
being bossy	sewing, mending
teaching manners	gardening
elegance	outside work/career

When they have finished, bring the groups back together; discuss their conclusions and find out whether there is any consensus.

Read the poem 'One-parent family' aloud to the class. Is it what they expected? Ask the children to explain the first stanza: *My mum says she's clueless...* How else might this have been expressed?

Talk with the children about the things that this mum can and can't do. Is she good at things they would expect a mum to be good at? What are these things? Leave room

for discussion of the many abilities of the children's own mums or female carers. Do any of them do unexpected jobs (such as builder or plumber) or have unexpected hobbies (such as football or carpentry)? Let the children think about women's jobs and careers, and the circumstances affecting mothers who go to work.

Encourage the children to think about dads. If a dad was the 'one parent', what would he have to learn to do? How would he manage? Explore the issues of traditional 'parent' roles and society's expectations. Ask the children whether they think these roles and attitudes are changing.

Give out copies of photocopiable page 127, and ask the children to read it through silently. Now ask them to say how the mother in the poem looks and dresses. What does it mean when the poet says: *She... / laughs at my disasters, says / that she's as bad...* What kind of 'disasters' might happen to the mother, or to the child? Why does the mother give 'a bad impression at the school'? What does this mean? How would mums and dads give 'a good impression' on Open Evenings, Sports Days and so on? Why would this be important to the child?

Read out the end of the last stanza again:

> ... 'Too bad,'
> the others sometimes say,
> 'you've got such a peculiar mum.'
> 'Just as well,' I tell them.
> 'She is my mother *and* my dad!'

Let the children discuss why 'the others' think that the speaker's mother is 'peculiar'. What do 'the others' think that word means? What does the speaker take it to mean? Why does he or she say 'It's just as well'? Discuss the way that this mother takes on the father's role as well as her own.

Now lead the children to consider the speaker, the 'I' in the poem. Is this the poet's own voice speaking? In a poem, the voice of the speaker is often used to communicate the poet's own words and ideas; but despite the use of 'I' or

'we', the speaker is often a character invented by the poet. What do the children think about the 'I' in this poem?

Break up the class into groups again, and ask the children to make notes for a poem about an invented character. They might think of an imaginary friend, a grandmother, a teacher, a neighbour, a shopkeeper... even a poet, perhaps! The children should keep these notes and use them to write a poem in a follow-up session.

Suggestion(s) for extension

Confident readers and writers can search through anthologies and collections to find similar poems which interest them. Suggest that they work in pairs to explore a poem, then set up a question and discussion session for others in the class. They should think about the feelings of the person or people in the poem, look for unusual descriptions of characters, note interesting words and phrases that characters have used, and so on.

Suggestion(s) for support

Children who need to be supported in reading and listening should work through this poem (or a similar one) in a small group, with an adult helper who will encourage them to explore their ideas.

Assessment opportunities

The children's contributions to the class discussions can be recorded (in writing or on cassette). Their understanding of the situation in which the mother finds herself will be apparent from their comments, as will their familiarity with the colloquial words and phrases used in the poem.

Display ideas

The children can use paints or felt-tipped pens to create portraits of the mother in 'One-parent family'. They should refer back to the poem for clues about how she dresses and what things she does. The paintings can be framed and hung gallery-style in the hall or corridor.

Reference to photocopiable sheet

The poem on photocopiable page 127 provides the focus for a wider discussion of the issues surrounding 'one-parent families'; this discussion should, in turn, lead the children to interpret the poem in more depth.

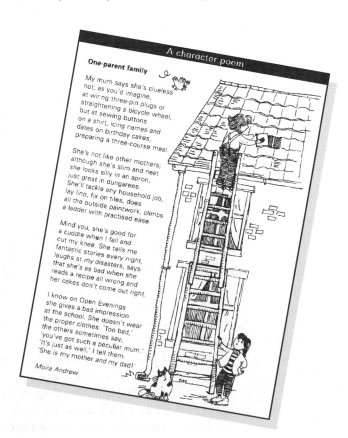

A character poem

One-parent family

My mum says she's clueless
not, as you'd imagine,
at wiring three-pin plugs or
straightening a bicycle wheel,
but at sewing buttons
on a shirt, icing names and
dates on birthday cakes,
preparing a three-course meal.

She's not like other mothers;
although she's slim and neat
she looks silly in an apron,
just great in dungarees.
She'll tackle any household job,
lay lino, fix on tiles, does
all the outside paintwork, climbs
a ladder with practised ease.

Mind you, she's good for
a cuddle when I fall and
cut my knee. She tells me
fantastic stories every night,
laughs at my disasters, says
that she's as bad when she
reads a recipe all wrong and
her cakes don't come out right.

I know on Open Evenings
she gives a bad impression
at the school. She doesn't wear
the proper clothes. 'Too bad,'
the others sometimes say,
'you've got such a peculiar mum.'
'It's just as well,' I tell them,
'She is my mother and my dad!'

Moira Andrew

Writing poems

When we ask children to write poetry in the classroom, we are doing this to develop their language skills in very specific ways. Children need to express their feelings, to describe things they see and hear, and to tell stories; poetry offers them opportunities to do all of these things.

From a child's point of view, writing a poem has the advantage of being a task which can be completed in one fairly short session. It does not usually need the concentrated planning of beginning, middle and end required for a story, and such drafting and rewriting as it demands is much quicker. Sometimes, 'low-achieving' children find that they are more able to write a poem, because it relies on a quick spurt of imagination rather than a sustained effort.

From a teacher's point of view, poetry is an ideal way of teaching many of the redrafting skills emphasized by the National Literacy Framework. It teaches children to look for 'the best words in the best order', and to edit out those which are unnecessary. Poetry writing also encourages children to take an individual look at the world, giving them reasons to make use of simile and metaphor.

Help children succeed by making poetry-writing a shared experience. Collect their ideas on the flip chart through brainstorming or 'shopping list' techniques. Model the drafting strategies: using arrows, crossing out, rewriting and so on. Encourage children to experiment with pattern and sound, including the use of rhythm and rhyme. Help them to appreciate when rhyme is appropriate and when it is not. As children come to understand the process of writing poetry, from the initial inspiration or brainstorming, through drafting and revising to final presentation, they will gain confidence in their ability to undertake and complete creative writing tasks.

POETRY

IMAGES OF THE MOON

To generate ideas by brainstorming, and go on to draft poems. To use simile and metaphor in poetry writing.

†† *Whole class, then individuals.*

🕐 *40 minutes.*

Previous skills/knowledge needed

This activity requires the children to listen, be imaginative and use language in a creative way. They should be able to recognize verbs and understand how to use them. They will need some experience of the process of drafting and the use of a thesaurus. They should be aware that some words can have the same meaning as others (or a closely similar meaning).

Key background knowledge

This activity is designed as an introduction to the use of image in the forms of simile and metaphor. It will encourage the children to explore how verbs work, and to use a wider vocabulary in order to express their imaginative ideas in vivid and unusual ways. You may find it useful to introduce the word 'synonym' for words which have the same meaning (or closely similar meanings).

The difference between simile and metaphor can be quite a subtle one:

▲ **Simile** involves direct comparison by means of an expression such as 'like', 'as green as' or 'as if'. 'This dragonfly is like a helicopter' is a simile.

▲ **Metaphor** identifies one thing with another for rhetorical effect, either blatantly (as in 'This dragonfly is a helicopter') or implicitly (as in 'The dragonfly's whirring propellers...'). Poets don't always tell the truth!

Preparation

It would be useful to check that the children remember how to use a thesaurus, and to consolidate their understanding of what verbs are. Make copies (one of each per child) of photocopiable pages 128 and 129. Find some other moon poems, such as 'Flying' by J.M. Westrup and 'The Oak and the Moon' by Catherine Benson (from *This Poem Doesn't Rhyme* edited by Gerard Benson, Puffin 1992). Obtain some moon pictures, as posters or in books. Make sure that anthologies or collections of poetry are available in the classroom.

Resources needed

Photocopiable pages 128 and 129; a flip chart; writing materials; a thesaurus for each group; pictures of the moon; moon poems (see above); black card, silver foil, silver pens, large paper clips, chalk; a range of poetry anthologies or collections.

What to do

Gather the children together as a class. Read out some poems about the moon. Without further discussion, ask the children to visualise the full moon. Can they 'see' the way it lights up the night sky and floats through the darkness?

Ask the children to choose a word to describe what the full moon does. List some of their suggestions in the middle of the flip chart. If these include 'shine', suggest that they find as many words as they can which mean the same thing. They may think of *glow, glitter, sparkle, gleam* and so on. Suggest that there is a way of finding more words, and ask the child who first thinks of using a thesaurus to look up 'shine' and scribe any words that have eluded them on the flip chart.

Now arrange the flip chart so that you have several synonyms for 'shine' listed with room to write a line underneath each one. Tell the children that they are going to 'think like poets' and find images for the moon. For example, if the moon *gleams*, what does it look like? The children might suggest that the moon *gleams like a pearl, like a mirror, like a polished pebble ...* and so on. Introduce the word *simile*, telling the children that when we use an image to say that one thing is like another, it is called a simile.

Take one of the children's similes for each verb, and show how the poem can be set out – for example:

The moon
    gleams
like a milky pearl
    shines
like a Hallowe'en lantern
    glows
like a candle flame

Now suggest that the children extend each of these similes, exploring the ideas of light and darkness which the images suggest. The poem will begin to grow in the following way:

Images of the moon
The moon
        gleams
like a milky pearl on a black dress
        shines
like a Hallowe'en lantern hanging from a tree
        glows
like a candle flame in a dark room

Point out that each single-word line uses a verb. Give out copies of the poem 'Moon thoughts' (photocopiable page 128) and give everyone a chance to read it silently. In this poem, the poet is more concerned with what the moon is like than with what it does, so she concentrates on the images rather than the verbs. Using the flip chart, and working from the children's suggestions, rewrite 'Moon thoughts' in the pattern of the poem above. The result might look like this:

> The moon
> > waits
> like a ripe pumpkin for Hallowe'en teeth,
> > glimmers
> like a lemon gumdrop almost sucked through,
> > tastes
> like a slice of lemon in a ginger beer sky,
> > shines
> like a brass button lost from a sailor's jacket.

The poet has thought of a set of images for the moon: *pumpkin, gumdrop, slice of lemon, watch, button.* Ask the children to find new images to fit in with the full moon – for example, *balloon, yo-yo, face, clock, lollipop* and so on. Use some of these new images to make up a new poem on the flip chart, with appropriate verbs each written in a single line (as above). The result might be:

Images of the moon

> The moon
> > flies
> like a silver balloon on a dark string,
> > dances
> up and down like a yellow yo-yo,
> > ticks
> like a white clock on a black wall,
> > smiles
> from the night like a clown's face.

Look at some of the moon pictures with the children. Note how the moon waxes and wanes, so that it has a different

shape at each stage of the month. Ask the children to find images to describe the moon when it has a crescent shape – for example, *boat, banana, mouth, hammock ...* If appropriate, you can introduce the word *metaphor* at this stage. Explain how a simile can be made into a metaphor by dropping the word 'like'. Thus the poem will look like this:

Images of the moon

> The moon is a boat
> > rocking
> on a dark sea.
> It is a banana
> > ripening
> in a black bowl.
> The moon is a mouth
> > smiling
> down on the world.
> It is a hammock
> > swinging
> between two tall trees.

Encourage the children to work orally on their crescent moon images, always finding an appropriate verb – for example, *The moon rocks/sails/bobs like a boat on the wild waves.*

Let the children return to their desks to work individually on their moon image poems. Give out copies of photocopiable page 129 for them to use as a writing frame. Emphasize that they should follow the solo-verb pattern as before. Give them time to work from word lists to a draft, then offer help with editing the final pieces. Encourage the use of appropriate verbs.

Finally, the children can present their moon poems by copying them out in silver pen on black circles of card. Each card circle can be backed with a slightly larger circle of silver foil (see Figure 1). Those who have finished can search through anthologies and collections for other moon poems, marking them with slips of paper for reading aloud or transcribing later. If the books are held open with large paper clips, they can be stood upright to display the poems on a 'moonscape' surface of silver foil with scattered shards of chalk.

Suggestion(s) for extension

More confident children could work on more image poems, such as 'Images of the Sun', 'Images of Space', 'Images of the Sea' or 'Images of the Wind'. They should follow the same procedure, working from a set of verbs. A wind poem might start from the sounds it makes – for example: *The wind / howls / like a ghost in the night, / roars / like a tiger in a cage, / whispers / like autumn leaves falling to the ground.*

Some of the children might use metaphor instead of

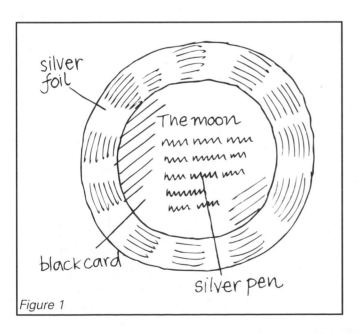

silver foil

The moon

black card

silver pen

Figure 1

simile, so that the poem could become, for example, *The wind is a ghost / howling / in the night. / It is a tiger / roaring / from its cage...* and so on.

Children who have found new poems about the moon in the class poetry books might try altering them to match the solo-verb pattern which they have been practising.

Suggestion(s) for support

If a child lacks the range of vocabulary needed to work independently on this task, arrange for him or her to work in a pair with a more able child. The pair can start by creating a list of simple moon images from which to work – for example:

▲ toys: *ball, balloon*
▲ flowers: *daisy, white rose*

From such a list, it will be easy for them to construct an image poem about the moon by describing how a ball or balloon moves, what a daisy or rose does, and so on. Encourage the use of photocopiable page 129 for this purpose. A typical result might be:

> The moon
> bounces
> like a ball in the park,
> floats
> like a balloon in the air,
> grows
> like a daisy in the grass,
> opens
> like a white rose in the garden.

Assessment opportunities

Note the children who can find images and use them in the form of similes and metaphors; who can understand how a verb functions in a sentence; and who can find and use synonyms for a verb with confidence.

Opportunities for IT

The children should be shown how to use an electronic thesaurus – either one connected to a word processor, or a dedicated computer or portable hand-held thesaurus. Children with access to palmtop computers may find that there is a thesaurus already included.

You could set up a writing frame of the moon poem using a word processor, and then save it as a file. The children could then retrieve this file and use it as the basis for their own poem, writing directly onto the computer. Alternatively, the children could originate their poem on a word processor, print it and then save their poem to disk. Further redrafting could be carried out on a printed copy. The children could then return to the computer to retrieve and edit their original poem before printing out a final copy.

Display ideas

An idea for the visual presentation of the children's poems is included in 'What to do' above. In addition, the children could make up new moon poems and present them in the same way (on circles of black card with a silver foil surround). A group of such 'moons' can then be connected together with threads and wooden batons or skewers, and hung as a mobile (if this can be done with safety).

Reference to photocopiable sheets

Photocopiable page 128 presents a poem based on images, which can be used as a stimulus for work on different ways of writing an image: as a simile, as a metaphor, using different verbs and so on. Photocopiable page 129 provides a writing frame to help children write 'moon poems' which employ similes.

A POEM IS...

To write verses for a group poem based on a repetitive starting point.

†† *Whole class, then group and individual work.*

🕐 *45 minutes.*

Previous skills/knowledge needed

It will be useful for the children to have some experience of brainstorming and listing. They should be used to sharing their ideas, and be familiar with the drafting process.

Key background information

This activity is a familiar starting point for poetry writing. The kind of poem developed here is one of the easiest to write, and gives confidence to those who say they don't know where to start! It can also be used as a building block for children who are ready for some quite ambitious work, giving them a way to work fairly profound thoughts and ideas into their writing. Your task is to judge where the children are in terms of their development as poets, and to use this activity as a vehicle to develop their talents at all levels of achievement.

Preparation

Make one copy per child of photocopiable page 130. Find some short poems of the 'Love is ...'/'Happiness is ...'/ 'Sadness is ...' type as back-up. For example, see 'The word is ...' by Ian Souter (from *Crack Another Yolk* edited by John Foster, OUP 1996); 'What is peace?' by Moira Andrew (from *Dove on the Roof* edited by Jennifer Curry, Methuen 1992); 'Blue is a lake' by Mary O'Neill (from *The First Lick of the Lolly* edited by Moira Andrew (Macmillan Ed. 1986); 'The Children's Carol' by Eleanor Farjeon (from *Poetry Corner 2*, BBC 1993). If possible, obtain a copy of the poem 'Don't' by Richard Edwards (from *The Word Party*, Lutterworth Press 1986, or from *Read a Poem/Write a Poem* edited by Wes Magee, Blackwell 1989) for reading aloud.

Resources needed

Examples of 'definition' poems (see above); anthologies and collections of poetry; a board or flip chart; writing materials, felt-tipped pens; photocopiable page 130; 'Don't' by Richard Edwards (see above).

What to do

Organize a brainstorming session for the whole class. Ask the children to think about a poem – any poem they know. Can anyone remember words or lines to share with the others? (There will be a stunned silence for a minute or two!) Then ask them to say what they think a poem is. They must begin with the words: *A poem is* ... They may suggest: *A poem is a lot of words strung together. A poem is some ideas put into lines on a page. A poem is words*

that rhyme. Always? *A poem is words that sometimes rhyme.*

Encourage the children to think more deeply, asking not only what a poem is on the page, but what it can do for the reader. *A poem is words that make you laugh or make you cry. A poem is a way of painting pictures in your head...* and so on. Scribe some of these ideas on the flip chart and divide each suggestion into two lines – for example:

A poem is words that can
make you laugh and make you cry.
A poem is a way of
painting pictures in your head.
A poem is a lot of words
standing in line on a page.
A poem is special writing when
 you don't want to write too much...

Read aloud some of the poems suggested in 'Preparation' above, and discuss with the children how a pattern is established in each.

Divide the children into groups. Give each child a copy of photocopiable page 130, and suggest that they make up a 'definition' poem from one of the topics on the sheet. Suppose they choose 'Night is ...' for example. Each member of the group should take it in turn to make up a line, such as:

▲ *Night is when you're sent to bed.*
▲ *Night is when the wardrobe goes walking.*
▲ *Night is when dreams come.*
▲ *Night is when the moon goes sailing.*

At this stage, all the work should be oral. Then the children should work together to draft out a group poem. Suggest that each Night idea should be extended so that it will make two lines when put into writing. Each child can use photocopiable page 130 to draft an idea. Make sure that this is a group activity in which all the children participate. They should be encouraged to discuss their lines and decide whether they want to make any changes. Then they should write out their poem, putting the lines in the best order. It might begin to look like this:

Night is when you're sent to bed
and downstairs the grown-ups are laughing.
Night is when the wardrobe goes walking
and shadows dance across the floor.
Night is when dreams come floating
behind your eyes and into your head.
Night is when the moon goes sailing
across the dark like a silver ship.

When each group has finished, they should read their poem aloud to the class.

Suggest that the children move on to work on individual

POETRY

pieces of writing, choosing another topic from photocopiable page 130 and working on it in a similar way. Some children may already be familiar with the use of metaphor and be keen to develop the simple list poem suggested above into an image poem – for example:

Night is an empty box
rolling in space forever.
Night is a black velvet cloak
wrapped around the stars.

A good follow-up to this activity is to base a repetitive poem on a word such as 'Don't!' Discuss with the children the many phrases that adults use which begin with 'Don't!' Collect a selection of these familiar phrases: *Don't slide down the banisters! Don't talk with your mouth full! Don't scowl at Auntie Ruth! Don't go splashing in the puddles! Don't get your new sweatshirt in a mess!* and so on – forever!

Read Richard Edwards' poem 'Don't' with the class (if possible). Listen to the chorus:

Why do people say 'don't' so much,
Whenever you try something new?
It's more fun doing than don'ting,
So why don't people say 'do'?

Encourage the children to discuss how the poet feels about 'don'ting', and ask them to use the methods they have practised to create a 'dos and don'ts' poem. Remind them to start by compiling a list – perhaps first grouping together all the 'don'ts' connected with bedtimes or meals. They should then write the individual lines and arrange them in a sequence, taking care to read them over and check that that they 'sound right' (for example, that the rhythm is consistent). Suggest that they might work on a chorus to 'top' and 'tail' their poem, as Richard Edwards has done.

Suggestion(s) for extension

More able children could use repetitive line starters of a more ambitious kind – for example, making a poem from a series of questions beginning with *Why? Who? What?* or *Where?* (See

'Who?' and 'Where?' from *Morning Break* by Wes Magee, CUP 1989.) They might imagine a familiar scenario from home or school, with an adult asking typical repetitive questions:

'Where?' asked my mother,
'is your new blue tee-shirt?'
I looked at the floor
and pretended I'd never
ever cleaned my bike with it.
'Where?' asked my father,
'is my yellow-handled screwdriver?'
I ....
....
....

... and so on, with each question in two lines and the child's response in three short lines.

Another extension task might be to make up a poem of three or four verses, each of which begins with the same weather phrase – for example:

When the sun shines
children like to chase shadows.
When the sun shines
grandmas like to sit in the shade.
When the sun shines
babies like to... and so on.

When they have worked through a suitable model, the children can create pieces where each two-line verse begins with the words: *When the fog drifts... When the snow falls... When the wind blows...* (See 'When the wind blows' from *Four O'Clock Friday* by John Foster, OUP 1991.)

Figure 2

Figure 3

More confident children can also be encouraged to work on extended list poems, using topics they have chosen.

Suggestion(s) for support
The first activity in 'What to do' is designed to give confidence to less able writers. They should concentrate on using photocopiable page 130 to create one-line or two-line pieces, for example:

> School is sitting still
> and writing a poem.
> School is running around
> when the bell rings.

As well as the examples given on page 130, the children could try colours: *Gold is... Red is... Blue is... Silver is...* and so on. (See 'Colour Story – from Gold to Silver' in *Four O'Clock Friday* by John Foster, OUP 1991.)

Assessment opportunities
Note the children who can move on from simple listing to creating poems with more depth. Look for those whose vocabulary is exciting, and who can use the redrafting process to good effect.

Opportunities for IT
Some children may like to originate and redraft their poem using a word processor. In order to reduce the typing time, you could set up several poem frames with the key lines (for example, *Night is...*) already entered. These could be saved to disk under different file names, so that the children can retrieve an appropriate file and work directly onto the computer. This might be particularly useful for children needing support, as the structure is clearly identified for them.

Final poems could be illustrated with clip art, or with pictures created in an art package or scanned from the children's own line drawings. A 'Night is...' poem could be set against a night-time background, with the text produced in a white font.

Display ideas
The children could write with silver pens on a black or dark blue background to display their poems about Night. They could write their 'A poem is...' poems on cards shaped like open books and display them against a painted background of book spines, looking as if they were on a bookshelf (see Figure 2).

On or near Valentine's Day, suggest that children write short 'Love is...' poems (*Love is washing up the breakfast dishes for my mum... Love is not making muddy footprints all over the kitchen floor... Love is when my dad takes me to a football match*). Suggest that each child write out his or her poem on a red heart. You can then hang the hearts on a tall cut-out tree to make a Valentine tree of love poems (see Figure 3).

Performance ideas
The children can read a cluster of 'definition' poems on different topics aloud, after rehearsal. They may wish to memorize and recite them. 'Don't' or 'Where?' poems can lead to some very effective role-play.

Reference to photocopiable sheet
Photocopiable page 130 provides some starting points for work on poems which use repeated line openings such as 'Night is...' or 'Don't...'. This sheet can be used by children to compose verses for inclusion in a group poem, or to compose individual two-line or four-line poems (see 'Suggestion(s) for support').

COLOUR ME BLUE

To use descriptive images of colour in a poem to evoke a mood.

†† *Pairs, then individual work.*

🕐 *40 minutes.*

Previous skills/knowledge needed

The children should have some experience of the drafting process, and need to be confident about sharing their feelings with others in the class. They will benefit from having previously discussed colours in the context of artwork.

Key background information

This activity is designed to explore the children's feelings and emotions, and needs to be handled sensitively. Watch for children who appear uneasy about sharing their thoughts, and be ready to intervene where necessary.

Preparation

Bring in some colour charts of the kind that a painter or decorator might use, as well as some objects and pictures as listed below. Obtain recordings of two contrasting pieces of music, such as Handel's *Music for the Royal Fireworks* and Mendelssohn's *Fingal's Cave Overture*.

Resources needed

Colour charts; a variety of objects in different colours (for example, a silk scarf, a decorated jug or dish, glass marbles, pine cones, shells); a board or flip chart; writing materials; a colour photograph or painting of a 'green' scene; CDs or cassettes of contrasting pieces of music.

What to do

Ask the children to name all the different colours they can think of. They will usually begin with the primary colours and then move on to more unusual ones, such as turquoise, crimson, silver, violet and ebony. Ask a couple of children to keep count by making a tally on the flip chart (see Figure 4). Talk a little about 'cold' and 'hot' colours, suggesting that different colours can influence people's moods.

Encourage the children to look at and handle some of the objects you have brought into the classroom. Can they classify these objects by colour? Ask helpful questions, such as: *Do the shells and feathers go into the same set? What about pine cones and driftwood? Buttercups and bananas?*

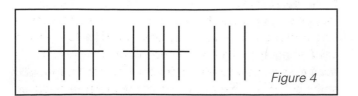

Figure 4

Should a turquoise brooch go into the green set or the blue set?

Show the children the 'green' photograph or painting. Focus their attention on the range and variety of one colour: green alone is like a paintbox! Encourage them to look out of the window at the trees, hedges and grass (if any). What different greens can they see? Establish that every colour has many different shades. Look at the range of greens on the painter's chart, and talk about some of the exciting names that paint manufacturers use: *jade, emerald, jungle green, sage, bottle green, leaf green, olive* and so on.

Organize the class into pairs. Each child will need paper and a pencil. Ask them to choose a colour and write down how it makes them feel, keeping their ideas secret. When everyone has finished, ask them to read out the clues to their partners, who should try to guess the colours. A typical clue might be:

A sad colour. Makes me think of winter-time, cold fingers and icy toes. It has a silky feel to it. It also belongs to the sea and sky. It makes me feel shivery. *(Blue)*

After all the children have exchanged clues, ask those who got the right answers how they guessed. Now get all the children who wrote about the colour blue to read out their ideas. Then do the same for other colours. Use the flip chart to make a note of all the 'feeling words' which the children have suggested, for example:

▲ Blue: sad, silky, cold, unhappy, lonely.

▲ Red: hot, spiky, angry, cross, dangerous.

Discuss with the children why the colours they chose made them think of the clues they used. Spend a few minutes listening and exchanging thoughts about feelings and emotions.

Ask the children to listen with care to two pieces of music – for example, part of *Fingal's Cave* and a section from *The Royal Fireworks*. Do not reveal the titles. Ask them to guess which piece (in this case) described the sea. Encourage them to talk about how it made them feel and what colours the music suggested. Discuss the effect of the 'fireworks' music: the shapes and colours the children imagined.

Suggest that poetry, like music, can evoke colours and feelings. Ask the children to look back at the colour clues they wrote earlier in the activity and add some more ideas – for example, thinking of flowers, weather, fruit or things around us that are usually that colour. Ask them to think again about how the colour makes them feel, and to add more feelings to their original notes.

From these notes, the children should then draft a colour poem in seven or eight lines, adding and taking out ideas until they are happy with the result. Tell them that they should try to paint a picture in words. They might achieve something like the following:

Blue

Blue is a lake, a river,
deep underwater caves.
It is shivery,
the colour of winter,
of sadness, silky as
a cool wind twirling
its scarf of misty air
around bare branches.

Children who finish this task successfully might write another colour poem based only on what they can see from the classroom window or from looking at a book illustration or a poster.

Suggestion(s) for extension

More accomplished writers can gather and use a set of words for a single colour, perhaps using a painter's or decorator's chart as before. For 'blue', for example, they might suggest: *indigo, pale blue, sky blue, peacock, cornflower, royal blue, ultramarine, moody blue, azure...* They should put these colour words together in a rhythmic way – for example:

A thousand blues in the sea,
peacock, ultramarine,
sky blue, sapphire,
turquoise, midnight,
moody blue, cobalt,
a thousand blues in the sea.

Or again, by using a seed guide to catalogue all the blue flowers in the garden:

A hundred blues in the garden,
bluebell, hyacinth,
cornflower, gentian,
sea-holly, lavender,
forget-me-not, flax,
a hundred blues in the garden.

They might like to use colour words to set a scene and suggest a mood, as in this extract from a poem by Moira Andrew:

Blue flowers stand tall
in a blue bowl, splashing the walls
with summer shadow.
Day dies, grey light
filters through open doors until
the first petal falls.

Another possible extension task for more capable writers is to work on a 'days of the week' colour poem such as the following:

Monday is a blue day,
Tuesday's painted white,
Wednesday's grey as feathers,
Thursday purple as night.
Friday is a gorgeous green,
Saturday lipstick-red,
Sunday is sun-bright yellow
Till it's time to go to bed.

This example rhymes, but the poem doesn't need to – for instance:

I feel quite blue on Monday,
On Tuesday I'm sad and white.
I'm lonely and grey on Wednesday,
On Thursday I'm black and cross.
I'm a friendly green on Fridays,
On Saturday I'm a fiery red.
On Sundays I'm good and shine
all day like the golden sun.

Suggestion(s) for support

Children who find writing difficult could also try a 'days of the week' colour poem, keeping it very simple – for example:

Monday is blue and sad.
Tuesday is pink and jolly.
Wednesday is grey and lonely.
Thursday is yellow and bright.
Friday is green and friendly.
Saturday is orange and happy.
Sunday is silver and quiet.

Assessment opportunities

Note the children who are ready to take part in the preliminary oral work, and those who can share their feelings through writing and discussion. Look for children who display a wide vocabulary, knowing, understanding and adding to a range of unusual colour words.

Opportunities for IT

The completed colour poems could be presented using a word processor or desktop publishing package, with each of the lines printed in a different shade of blue. The teacher may need to ensure that the computer is using a multi-colour mode (256 colours at least) in order to give the children enough shades to chose from. The children will need to know how to select different font colours, and (with some software) how to use the colour picker to select an

appropriate shade. This is often accessed using the *'more colours'* option. In poems where the children have used different colour words, they could try to match up each colour word to an appropriate colour shade.

The children could also present their poems on a colour background – possibly produced using an art package which allows colour blending or washes. This would allow them to use a range of shades, as in a sunset background. They could then experiment with different font colours to make the poem stand out against the coloured background. You may need to consider the cost of using this kind of background colour printing for a whole class!

Display ideas
The children can make an appropriate coloured-pencil backing for their colour poems. This should be done very faintly, so that the written work is not obscured. Where they have suggested a range of words for a single colour, the children can make a wavy striped background, varying the shade and tint very slightly from one stripe to the next.

WHAT CAN I DO WITH IT?

To develop the ability to write imaginatively, using close observation and figurative language. To consolidate the ideas of simile and metaphor.

†† *Whole class, then groups of six and individual work.*
🕐 *45 minutes*

Previous skills/knowledge needed
The children should be familiar with drafting and editing techniques. They should have had practice in group work and sharing ideas. They should know what **simile** and **metaphor** mean, and understand the difference between them.

Key background information
This activity requires an 'imaginative leap' on the part of the child, who needs to look at familiar objects in a new way: not as actual things (which are), but as potential things (which might be). They also need to be able to visualize new uses for objects which they usually take for granted. Simile and metaphor are discussed in 'Images of the moon' (page 48).

Preparation
Make one copy per child of photocopiable pages 131, 132 and 133. Obtain a small glass (coloured) marble. Bring in a range of objects for use as writing stimuli:
▲ some quite ordinary things which could be viewed in extraordinary ways, such as a pencil sharpener, a board duster, an old tennis ball, a spider plant, a plastic flower

pot, shells, pebbles, acorns, catkins and so on;
▲ some strange-looking objects, such as a broken umbrella, a gnarled root, a rusted lock, a fossil or a lump of amethyst. You could also provide some things from the past, such as a tattered fan, an old shoe or a pocket watch; or some things from other countries. The objects themselves are not important: it is what the children can imagine about them that matters.

Resources needed
A collection of objects (see above); photocopiable pages 131, 132 and 133; writing materials; a board or flip chart; a glass marble.

What to do
Introduce the activity by taking a few minutes to play the 'What if...?' game. What if you wanted to play football and didn't have goalposts: what would you use? If you needed a hammer and didn't have one? If you wanted to stir your tea, but didn't have a spoon? Establish that many objects have possible uses other than those intended.

When you have tried out a few ideas (the more outlandish the better), suggest that the children are going to take a 'sideways' look at some everyday objects. Discuss what this might mean. Tell them that poets often work this way, turning ordinary things into extraordinary ones. Read Judith Nicholls' poem 'What Can You Do With A Pencil?' (photocopiable page 131) together. Take time to discuss what the poet has done here. How do the children think she came to imagine the pencil as a lollystick, a teaspoon, a chopstick and so on? Was it the pencil's shape? Was it through actually trying to use it in these ways? Ask the children to think of some more new ways of using a pencil.

Ask the children to look at something else found in a classroom in this way – for example, a pencil sharpener or a board duster. Encourage them to work orally at this stage. Read Moira Andrew's poem 'Ten things to do with a frisbee' (photocopiable page 132) with them. This is like the pencil poem, but concentrates on different words for flying: *spin, whizz, zip* and so on.

Once the children have had a few minutes' practice at 'looking through a poet's eyes', tell them that you have a puzzle for them. Say that you have something hidden in your hand, and that you will give them a poet's clues about what it is. When they think they know, they should put their hands up but keep quiet. Tell the children that the object is like:

> a small round sun
> a shining eyeball
> a trapped sunbeam
> a mini-world
> a boiled sweet
> a coloured pebble... and so on.

After they have had a few guesses, open your hand to reveal a glass marble. Now ask the children to think of other things that the marble looks like. Use the flip chart to create a list poem from their suggestions. This could be written out in question form – for example:

What is the secret I hold in my hand?
Is it a small round sun shining?
Is it a monster eyeball staring?
Is it a sunbeam trapped in a jar?
Is it a mini-world spinning in space?
Is it a boiled sweet sucked almost dry?
Is it a pebble washed by the sea?
Look! It's a marble I hide in my hand.

Now give each group a different object. Remind them that it doesn't matter whether or not they know what the object 'really' is. They must imagine what it would look like to them if they didn't know anything about it. Suggest that they each say what they think it is *like* – for example, a broken umbrella is like a stork's legs, like a skeleton's ribs, and so on. Remind the children that these images are *similes*: they suggest that one thing is like another.

Each group should rough out their ideas, then choose the best similes – one to a line. They should then arrange their lines in the best order. They can turn the ideas into a list of questions like those on the flip chart, building them into a 'riddle' or 'secret' poem. After a few minutes, ask the groups to read out their poems a line at a time. The others should try to guess what the secret object was.

Now take an object, such as a silver pocket watch. Examine it in the closed state, and write some appropriate similes on the flip chart: *like a full moon, like a silver eye.* Then half-open the watch case and observe that it looks like a flower opening, like a silver butterfly, and so on. Write

The old pocket watch
Closed, it is a full moon
shining from the dark.
It is a silver eye
staring from a stranger's face.
Open, it is a summer flower
blooming in the sun.
It is a sparkling butterfly
fluttering over the garden.
But the old pocket watch has stopped,
keeping safe the secrets of time.

out the poem as a descriptive piece, asking the children to add new ideas to 'colour' the draft (see below left). Remind the children that this poem, though still relying on image, uses metaphor instead of simile. The word 'like' has been dropped. Ask them what effect they think this has had on the power of the images.

When this class poem has been redrafted and polished, suggest that the children choose another object to write about, either in groups or individually. They can either use the secret/riddle technique or write a descriptive poem like 'The old pocket watch'. They can use either simile or metaphor to express the 'imaginative leap'.

Suggestion(s) for extension
Ask the more experienced writers to use 'Ten things to do with a frisbee' by Moira Andrew (photocopiable page 132) as a basis for a copycat poem about another toy – for example, describing ten things to do with a kite, a ball or a skipping rope. Alternatively, they could find new uses for classroom utensils such as an elastic band, a tape measure or a ruler. Suggest that they start off gently, then let their imaginations run free – for example:

Things to do with a kite
You can fly it over the hill,
catch it in the topmost branch
of the tallest tree.
You can twirl it round your hand,
lead it into darkest space
like a green and yellow dog.
You can ride it through the air,
see what it's like on the other side
of the world...

More confident writers could also be encouraged to extend their use of simile and/or metaphor. They could think of a flying object such as a frisbee, a kite or a paper aeroplane, then list various images for it – for example, *a paper aeroplane is like an arrow, a dart, a harpoon, a ribbon, a white bird* and so on. They should build on these images to write a poem, using either simile or metaphor, as in the following examples:

A paper aeroplane
flies across the classroom
like a poisoned dart
It speeds through the air
like a super-charged arrow.   *(Simile)*

POETRY

A paper aeroplane
is a poisoned dart
flying across the classroom.
It is a super-charged arrow
speeding through the air.   *(Metaphor)*

Suggestion(s) for support

With children who need support, choose a familiar object with lots of possibilities. For example, if you choose a piece of string, give them a small piece each and help them by asking questions: *What would you do with the string if you had a parcel? Can you remember making patterns with string?* and so on. Write down each answer on a slip of paper, then help the children to put these ideas in the best order. This becomes something of a game, out of which a group poem will emerge:

> Things to do with a piece of string
> You can tie Granny's parcel with it.
> You can play a game with the cat.
> You can make paint patterns with it.
> You can keep the house key on it.
> You can measure things with it.

Assessment opportunities

Note the group reaction while ideas are being exchanged and poems built up. Look for those who can make the imaginative leap necessary to visualize new possibilities for familiar objects. These are the children who will be able

to think of imaginative similes and metaphors when they come to write their own descriptive poems.

Opportunities for IT

The children could use a multi-media authoring package to make an interactive display of their completed 'secret' poems. Each child or pair should be given two pages of the presentation to use. On the first page, they should write their poem. It may already have been written using a word processor, in which case it can be inserted onto the page without retyping it. The children can format their text to make it look interesting, and change the font style and size to fill the page. They should be careful about adding pictures that might give the secret away. The second page should contain the 'answer'. This could be either a word or a suitable picture.

The children then need to link the answer page to the 'secret' poem – perhaps by placing a large question mark on the page which functions as an icon: when you click on it, you are shown the answer page. The children could extend the activity by adding a spoken version of their riddle, recorded using a microphone attached to the computer; the riddle page could have an ear or other symbol which the user should click on in order to hear the riddle.

Older or more able children could arrange for a new line to appear each time the user clicks on the page, so that the whole poem does not appear in one go. They could even add a space for the user to type what he or she thinks is the answer. An incorrect answer will cause another line of the poem to appear; a correct answer will be rewarded with the rest of the poem and/or the answer page. (See 'Riddles' in Chapter 4, page 100.)

Display ideas

The children's 'secret' poems can be displayed using photocopiable page 133 (perhaps copied onto card). As Figure 5 shows, each child should:
▲ fold a copy of the sheet in four;
▲ write the poem on the inside;
▲ sign the title page on the outside;
▲ cut a flap to hide the answer.

Reference to photocopiable sheets

Photocopiable pages 131 and 132 present imaginative 'list' poems which the children can use as stimuli when creating their own similar poems, and when working on the concepts of simile and metaphor. Photocopiable page 133 can be folded, cut and written on by the child to create a 'secret poem' display.

Figure 5

A list poem (1)

What Can You Do With A Pencil?
(For an unknown; bay in Winchester)

You can sharpen it
or break the point,
trap it in the door;
fasten it behind your ear
or *tap* it on the floor;
use it as a walking stick
(if you're very small),
dig a hole to plant a seed,
tap it on a wall;
use it as a handy splint
for rabbits' broken legs;
stir your coffee,
stir your tea,
stir up all the dregs!
Drop it from a table top,
pop it in a case;
use it as a lollystick,
send it up in space!
Two will give you chopsticks,
one could pick a lock;
bore a hole and thread one
to darn a hole-y sock...

These are just a few ideas,
there must be *hundreds* more...
but meantime, trap it, snap it, flap it,

TAP IT ON THE FLOOR!

Judith Nicholls

A list poem (2)

Ten things to do with a frisbee

You can spin it in the air.
You can whizz it across a chair.

You can send it into space.
You can enter it in a race.

You can fly it above the trees.
You can float it on the breeze.

You can zip it across the sky.
You can make it soar up very high.

You can fling it over the river
Help! You've lost track of it forever!

Moira Andrew

A secret poem

by _____

Fold

What's my secret?

What's my secret?

_____
_____
_____
_____
_____

Fold

Lift the flap to find out.

A RIVER OF WORDS

To explore word associations. To experiment with the sounds of words – including rhyme, rhythm and cadence – in order to produce a polished poem through redrafting.

†† *Whole class, then pairs, then individual work.*

🕐 *45 minutes.*

Previous skills/knowledge needed

This activity needs quick wits and the ability to associate words freely without a need for explanation. The children should feel confident about sharing ideas and using words to explore experience. They should have some drafting skills and be able to 'think on their feet', exchanging words in rapid-fire dialogue.

Key background information

This activity explores the idea of using words for their sounds and the sensory impressions they evoke. Ideally, the words should flow spontaneously onto paper from the children's initial brainstorm; this should lead to a more sober editing session in which the teacher is a facilitator, helping the children to choose the 'best words in the best order' for the finished piece.

Preparation

Make one copy of photocopiable page 134, enlarged to A3 size) on card. Cut it up into individual word cards. Obtain a stop-watch or stop-clock.

Resources needed

A board or flip chart; writing materials; word cards from photocopiable page 134; dictionaries; a stop-watch.

What to do

Divide the class into pairs, and tell them that you are going to hold an 'auction sale' of words. This will involve choosing a stimulus card and selling it off at the highest price – that is, for the greatest number of related words. The word printed on the card should start the children thinking of other words that go with it – not meaning the same, but being connected to it in some way. The connected words should pour out in a continuous stream – a 'river of words'.

To show the children how to go about this exercise, take one word card. Display it and tell the children that they should try to come up with one word which goes with it, then another word which goes with the second one, and so on. Encourage them to respond very rapidly, almost without thinking. Insist that the children take turns, and make this a fast oral game. Starting with FOREST, for example, which might lead to: *forest, tree, leaf, green, grass, daisy, summer, sun, butterfly, wings, flying, balloon,*

POETRY

high, sigh, cry, sad, blue, sky, cloud, rain...

The different kinds of link are worth looking at. Usually one word will link up with the next in an obvious thematic way, as in *summer, sun, butterfly*. Occasionally the sound of a word will give the link, as in *high, sigh, cry*. Sometimes feelings may make new word associations, as in *cry, sad, blue*. The children should be reassured that anything goes!

After the excitement of this initial 'word river', take a different card and follow the same procedure. When everyone has had a turn at contributing a word, scribe the complete 'river' of related words on the flip chart, ready for the next step.

In the meantime, the pairs of children should each have a word card to work on. Ask them to take turns to add a word, creating a 'word river' between them and writing it down. Tell them that they have five minutes to tackle this, and set the stop-watch. When they have finished, ask the children to read out their word rivers. Make a count, and see which pair has thought up the longest chain of related words.

Now work from the flip chart and, with the children's help, make up a short poem, using as many of the associated words as possible. You can add further words as you go along. Complete sentences are not necessary, but you need to be aware of cadence and rhythm. As an example, here are two verses derived from the 'forest' word association:

> Summer sun,
> blue sky,
> fragile butterflies
> flying high.

> Autumn cloud,
> winds cry,
> ash-white clouds.
> Sad, I sigh.

There may not be much of the 'forest' in this piece, but the poem works – mainly because of the rhymes that were available in the original 'word river'.

Let the children try out different responses, using the same 'river of words'. They can use plurals, change the tenses of verbs and so on, as in the following piece:

First days of autumn

> Trees wave and the forest sighs,
> shadows dance until a leaf falls
> and green sadly turns to brown.
> Butterflies fly like blue balloons
> until wings of cloud bring rain.
> Trees wave and the forest cries.

Note how the unexpected juxtaposition of words gives this poem its distinctive voice: *until wings of cloud bring rain...* The poet may not have thought of this image before using the 'word river' to create the poem.

Now suggest that the children draft poems from the words they have collected for themselves. They may continue to write as a pair if they wish, but many will prefer to work as individuals. They should first plot out the available words in a suitable order, adding to and modifying the word list as the poem grows. Make dictionaries available for this work. Using the 'river of words', the children can move away from conventional ways of connecting words and let their ideas flow free.

Children who finish this task early can choose a different stimulus card, using it as the first word of their poem and building further lines out of associated words. For example, starting with STONE:

> Stone shore tides song
> Grey skies where gulls belong
> Wind water ships sails
> White waves where seaweed trails.

Emphasize that the poems don't have to be serious, and they can be just a few lines long. The important thing is that word association should unlock the child's imagination. Here is a more lightweight STONE poem:

Stone shoe foot hurts
Fall down, blood spurts.
Stone wall, sit and wait,
Mum come soon.
Please don't be late!

Suggest that when the children have completed their first drafts, they can try them out on their partners. Before they write their poems out in 'best', read them through and offer suggestions for editing and redrafting.

Suggestion(s) for extension

The most able children could try a slightly different approach to word association: focusing on the sounds and movements associated with a stimulus word such as RIVER, WATERFALL, STORM or MOTORWAY. For example:

Waterfall
Gushing, rushing,
  splashing, crashing,
    roaring, pouring,
      tumbling, bumbling,
        swirling, twirling,
          rushing, flushing,
            jetting, wetting!

Suggestion(s) for support

For children who lack confidence, look for words which suggest many possibilities for easy word-association, such as BEAR, SCHOOL, BREAKFAST or PLAYGROUND. Either scribe for the children or have them write down their set of words in a simple arrangement, four to a line. If they can work in a rhyme, so much the better – for example:

Breakfast
Cornflakes porridge juice milk
Jam marmalade coffee tea
Butter bacon eggs toast
It's bread and honey I like most!

Bear
Bear fluffy, night-time bed
Teddy cuddly, bow red.

Let these children read out their poems with the others. If they have difficulty reading aloud, do it for them; but let them bask in admiration of their work, like all the others.

Assessment opportunities

Note the children who are able to share their ideas and enjoy using words. Look for those who find it difficult to make word-associations, and even more difficult to make sense of a given selection of words.

Opportunities for IT

Children who are able typists could create their 'river of words' brainstorm using a word processor, placing each new word on a new line. An adult helper could act as a scribe for less proficient typists. The completed list could then be used as the basis for a poem. The children will need to know how to join words together using the *delete* key; how to mark and move words to a different place using *cut and paste* or *drag and drop* commands; and how to add new words to the text. Repeated lines should be copied and pasted into the new position, rather than being retyped.

Once the final version has been created, the children can experiment with different fonts, styles and formats to present their poem in an interesting way.

Display ideas

The children can create a 'river of words' frieze in dark blue, with the stimulus words cut out and pasted at the top (like rocks) and the poems which have been generated pasted off-centre beneath them (like currents in the water). Paint a few unsteady blue lines flowing over everything.

Reference to photocopiable sheet

Photocopiable page 134 should be duplicated onto card and cut up into individual word cards, which are used as stimuli for word-association.

BEACHCOMBER

To develop powers of description through careful choice of words and phrases, combining observation and imaginative use of language. To develop a poem through stages of construction and redrafting.

†† *Whole class, then paired or individual writing.*

🕐 *45 minutes.*

⚠ *Stress the dangers of 'beachcombing' in reality.*

Previous skills/knowledge needed

The children need to have a varied oral vocabulary, some ability in drafting and an understanding of the rhythms which help to make a poem effective. It would be helpful if they were familiar with the story of *Robinson Crusoe*.

Key background knowledge

This activity leads children to observe objects closely, in a scientific manner, and then to combine their observations with the descriptive and imaginative language of a poet. This activity could be tied in with a summer outing to a local beach – but it will work just as well with a bit of imagination on the part of the children and the teacher! Emphasize the dangers of picking up bits and pieces from the shore, and make sure that the children do this only under supervision (if at all).

Preparation

Bring in a basket containing various objects which might have been found on the shore, such as a piece of knotted rope, a glass float, driftwood, some shells, an old shoe, an empty bottle and so on. Obtain an illustrated version of *Robinson Crusoe* (or a similar castaway story). Make one copy per child of photocopiable pages 135 and 136.

Resources needed

A basket with 'found' objects (see above); a board or flip chart; writing materials; felt-tipped pens, scissors, adhesive; books telling the *Robinson Crusoe* story; photocopiable pages 135 and 136.

What to do

Introduce the activity by discussing recycling. The children should be aware of several materials which we, as a community, might be encouraged to save so that they can re-emerge in a new form: cans, glass products, newspapers and so on.

Ask whether anyone knows what a 'beachcomber' is. Explain that the word means a person who recycles bits and pieces found on the seashore. Discuss with the children the idea that a beachcomber needs to use his or her imagination to see the possible uses of what appears to be

worthless litter. The romantic image of a beachcomber is like that of a shipwrecked sailor, making use of various things washed up by the tides – as Robinson Crusoe does. Look together at an illustrated book of Robinson Crusoe's adventures. Ask the children what Crusoe might have found, and what uses he might have made of his findings. Encourage suggestions. If he had found some pieces of wood, what might he have done with them? Built a boat or a bed? Burned it as firewood? What about palm leaves: a fan to keep off the heat; a roof to keep out the rain? He might have used mussel shells as spoons, a coconut shell as a drinking cup and so on. Encourage a lively, imaginative session.

Produce the basket of 'found objects', taking out each object in turn and encouraging the children to describe its shape, colour and texture. If possible, include a piece of driftwood. Let them handle it, exploring its shape and texture. Read John Loveday's poem 'A driftwood pendant' (photocopiable page 135) together. Can they think of other things which could be carved from the driftwood?

Ask the children to describe the driftwood orally: *smooth, crooked, cream-coloured, with branches like fingers* and so on. Use the flip chart to list some of these descriptions under headings – for example:

▲ *looks like: a seaweed tree, a hand with fingers*
▲ *shape:*   *crooked, twisted, curly*
▲ *colour:*   *cream-coloured, pale brown, milky tea*
▲ *texture:* *smooth, sleek, slithery*

Now show the children how such a list can be used as the basis of a descriptive poem, with one line for each idea:

Driftwood

Washed smooth by the tides,
the driftwood is like a sleek hand
with seven crooked fingers,
pale as milky tea.

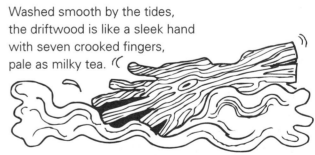

Encourage the children to choose a different found object, first noting its colour, texture and so on, then going on to draft a four- or five-line poem which describes the object in similar detail.

The next step is to ask the children to construct an imaginative story around the object which they have described. The story might suggest how the debris was left on the shore, who found it or what new object the castaway or beachcomber might make of it. Encourage the children to suggest unusual or fantastic outcomes.

Now ask the children, working in pairs or individually, to draft a longer poem based on one of the found objects. Suggest that they start, as before, with a description of the

object – its shape, colour and texture and so on – and then go on to imagine where it was found, why it was there and what use might be made of it. This allows a wide range of creative possibilities. For example, a child writing about a piece of driftwood might imagine it being carved into a magic bird:

> Whistling under his breath,
> the beachcomber works magic
> on the washed-up wood,
> carving, paring, turning
> until, at last, it becomes a bird
> trapped, fluttering, in his hands.

A poem about an empty bottle might focus on its possible source and intended purpose:

Bottle
Green as the deepest seas,
shiny, hard, glinting in the sun,
thrown overboard by a prisoner
to be shipwrecked on the shore.
A floating cry for help, its message
of terror corked tight inside
as, night and day, it rides the waves
to the other side of the world.

When the children have finished their draft poems, suggest that they share them with others in the class, reading them aloud if appropriate. Children who are too diffident to read out their work often find it helpful if an adult will do this for them.

The children can write their poems out in 'best' on the island outline on photocopiable page 136. They can draw, colour and cut out the found objects described in their poems, then stick them on around their written work.

Finish off the session by rereading 'A driftwood pendant'. The children can compare and contrast their own poems with this one by a 'professional' poet.

Suggestion(s) for extension
The more able children could write poems about Robinson Crusoe on his island, perhaps imagining him as a 'green' conservationist or a beachcomber expressing his ideas about the importance of recycling 'found' objects.

Suggestion(s) for support
Children who find the writing task difficult could write their poems as simple lists – for example:

On the shore we found
a knotted rope
twisted driftwood
pearl-white shells
a round float and
a green glass bottle.

Robinson Crusoe found
one old shoe
two knotted ropes
three empty bottles
four ragged nets
and five shiny shells.

Assessment opportunities
Note those children who can look closely at an object which is new to them, using a range of appropriate adjectives to describe it in a written poem with accuracy and flair.

Opportunities for IT
The children could use an art or drawing package to create their own imaginary island and mark on it where the different items have been washed up. Alternatively, they could use an art package to create a more detailed picture of one of the objects, perhaps using a real object as a model. The printed pictures could be used to illustrate a class book of 'beachcomber' poems produced using a word processor or desktop publishing package. One of the pictures could be used as the cover of the book.

A picture of the island with some found objects could also be used as the title page of a multi-media presentation of the children's poems. By clicking on one of the objects shown on the title page, the child would be taken to a page of poems about that particular object. Sound effects could be added – either recorded with a microphone attached to the computer, or recorded as sound sample files (for example, seagulls) from a suitable audio CD-ROM. The children could even include recordings of themselves reading their own poems.

Display ideas

Paint a background of a large island, showing a yellow shore, a blue sea, black mountains, green palm trees and so on. Ask the children to copy out their poems on plain paper, rough-cutting them around the edges, making them look crumpled and weather-beaten (but still legible). Stick the poems on the shoreline or in the water around the island. (See Figure 6.)

Performance ideas

The Robinson Crusoe story can be performed to an audience of other children in the school, with Crusoe displaying his beachcombing finds one by one and the poets reading their work as each 'treasure' is shown. The children might also script and record a news report about how Robinson Crusoe was rescued from his island. They should describe all the bizarre things that he has improvised from debris washed up on the shore and that he couldn't possibly leave behind!

Reference to photocopiable sheets

The poem on photocopiable page 135 can be used as a stimulus for children's poems about 'found' objects, their characteristics and their uses. The poem's sensitively observed detail provides a model of this kind of writing. Photocopiable page 136 is an 'island' picture which the children can use as a background for their 'found object' poems.

Figure 6

I'VE FOUND A POEM!

To write a 'found' poem, building on a non-fiction text.

†† *Whole class, then individual work.*

🕐 *45 minutes.*

Previous skills/knowledge needed

The children will need a Key Stage 2 level of skill in reading for information. They should be used to drafting and re-appraising their written work.

Key background information

'Found' poems are exactly what their name suggests. They are poems made from the text found in newspapers, on packets, in recipe or gardening books, on food labels, in

DIY instructions, and so on. 'Found' poems can arise anywhere – often in the most unlikely places. The children can rearrange the words they have found, add new ideas or leave bits out as they wish.

This activity requires a range of different kinds of reading matter, none of which is poetry. Printed information and instructions, letters, diaries, recipes and so on will prove very useful. Work on 'found' poetry fits well into an historical topic, since the activity will enhance the children's understanding of written materials from another generation.

Preparation

Encourage the children to bring from home some printed or written materials (as above) which come from the past. Arrange these on a History display table, along with appropriate books and posters. Alternatively, if you decide to use gardening-related materials, organize a display of gardening artefacts, seed packets, flower pots and relevant books. Likewise, if you decide to concentrate on recipes, design a simple cookery display table to display the texts. Make one copy per child of photocopiable pages 137 and 138. Bring in some empty seed packets.

Resources needed

Books, pictures and artefacts, as above; photocopiable pages 137 and 138 (the latter for support); an empty seed packet; a board or flip chart; coloured pens, writing materials, felt-tipped pens.

What to do

Working with the children as a class, give out copies of the poem 'Raspberry jam' by Moira Andrew (photocopiable page 137). Read the poem aloud. Stress the idea that, although it is written as a poem, this piece could also be used as a recipe. Encourage the children to point out the 'recipe words'. Scribe these on the flip chart:

Take 4lbs. of fruit.
Use whole clean berries.
Put in pan.
Add 4lbs. preserving sugar.
Bring slowly to the boil.
Keep to a full rolling boil
for five minutes only.
Pot up.

Suggest that the children look at the way in which the poet has added comments and details to enhance the recipe. Explore the poem with the children by asking questions and developing their replies: *Where did the recipe come from? Do you think it was old or new? What words or phrases give this away? Where did the raspberries come from? Who might have been in the kitchen with the poet? What did the jam look like when it was cooking? What did they do with the jam once it was ready?* and so on.

Tell the children that 'Raspberry jam' is a *found poem*. Can they explain why the word 'found' applies to it? Explain that this means that the poem started life as a different kind of writing – in this case, a recipe. A similar poem could have been 'found' in a letter, a newspaper, a diary or some instructions on how to heat up a pizza!

Suggest that they read 'Raspberry jam' for themselves, noting how the recipe has been chopped up into lines and the descriptive parts have been written around or between the bits of the recipe – for example, how the recipe was found on *a blue-lined pad*, the fruit is heaped *fragrant / into a great glass bowl* and, when the jam is almost ready, *The / heaving mass is pocked / with seed, darkens.*

Using the flip chart, show the children how to go about writing a found poem. Take a seed packet and read aloud its description of the flower and the sowing instructions – for example, a packet of Brachycome seeds says: *This profuse and long-flowering variety carries an abundance of delicately fragrant black or gold-centred daisy flowers throughout the summer months...* It goes on to give instructions for sowing: *Sow late winter... then... For summer-flowering pot plants, transplant the seedlings into*

POETRY

7.5cm pots. Keep cool and well-ventilated, and water freely.

Show the children how to extract phrases from the above text, filling in with their own words as they go along. The completed poem might be something like the following:

Sow the seeds in late winter,
when frost is icing the ground.
Transplant the tender seedlings
when the sun warms up the sky.
For summer flowering, plant
in cool pots. Water freely and
white daisy flowers will smile
from black gold-rimmed eyes,
winter remembered only in
their starry frosted petals.

Use different-coloured pens to demonstrate how the printed words and phrases are chopped up, and how appropriate description is added to develop the seed packet wording into a poem.

Give some empty seed packets to the children, and let them work individually. They should copy out the instructions they decide to use in the poem, chop them up, move them around and add their own pieces of descriptive writing.

Next, ask the children to draft poetic descriptions of the flowers in full bloom. The illustrations on the front of the seed packet will help them to think of ideas. The children need to mix and match instructional text and descriptive language, using arrows, crossing out and so on until a satisfactory poem emerges.

Help the children to edit their completed 'found' poems.

Suggestion(s) for extension

More confident writers could go on to choose a different non-fiction text from which to work. They might try recipes, newspaper cuttings or labels from tea or coffee packets, working in the same way with 'found' words and phrases allied to their own descriptive language.

They might also wish to choose a piece of text from the 'History' display (see 'Preparation' above), adding something about their feelings or describing the printed/written item (for example, a postcard or newspaper clipping) through their senses. This kind of writing adds a very personal dimension to the children's understanding of history.

Suggestion(s) for support

Those children who are unsure of their writing ability could start with the newspaper headlines on photocopiable page 138. Encourage them to think through ideas for a poem which might be found among the headlines. Let them cut up the words and move them around the table-top until they begin to make sense. Scribe the missing words which the children suggest, trying them in the gaps among the headlines until a group poem begins to grow. The result might look something like this:

The coldest night of the winter.
Snow like a white blanket
Thrown across the hills.
Frost sparkling in the forest
Like a silver wonderland.
But – children are in danger!
Iced-up lakes, dark deep waters.
Don't go out unless you must!

Encourage the children each to copy out a line in 'best' using a thick felt-tipped pen, and then to cut out their strips and glue them in order on a dark backing sheet. Finally, they can paint 'snow' falling over the finished poem.

Assessment opportunities

Note those children who can extract appropriate pieces of text and mix these with appropriate descriptive language. Look for the children who find this task very difficult, and suggest that they work from photocopiable page 138 (or find and use some current newspaper headlines).

Opportunities for IT

This is a good opportunity for children to use a prepared text on a word processor. The teacher could type in the instructions from a seed packet (for example) and save them onto a disk. The children could load this file into the word processor and develop their poem from the instructions. This will reduce the time needed for writing and allow the children to concentrate on the poem rather than the typing.

Figure 7

They will need to know how to:
▲ move around the text;
▲ edit and delete words;
▲ use the *Return* key to split lines;
▲ use the *Delete* key at the end of a line to join two lines together.

The *drag and drop* or *cut and paste* commands should also be taught, so that the children can move parts of the text around if they wish to.

Other starting texts could be prepared in a similar way. They could be typed in by you or by older pupils, taken as text from a suitable CD-ROM (this would be particularly useful for history topics), or scanned using an optical character recognition program (OCR). OCR software is supplied with most flatbed scanners; provided that the original text is in good condition, the scanned text can be converted accurately into editable word processor text. The children could even use their own word-processed non-fiction writing, which may already be saved on disk, as a starting text.

Display ideas
A display of printed and written texts connected to a theme such as 'History', 'Gardening' or 'Cooking' should be used to introduce this activity (see 'Preparation'), and left on the display table. Use streamers to connect the original texts to the subsequent 'found' poems displayed on a backing frieze above the table (see Figure 7).

Reference to photocopiable sheets
Photocopiable page 137 presents an example of a 'found' poem which adds descriptive imagery to pieces of an instructional text. Photocopiable page 138 presents five related newspaper headlines; children who have difficulty with the 'found poem' idea could use this page as a simple source of words to put together a 'found poem' on the theme of winter.

POETRY

BOX OF DREAMS

To write a poem in response to a specific stimulus, using images derived from sensory experience and paying particular attention to rhythm.

†† *Whole class, groups, then individual work.*

🕐 *45 minutes.*

Previous skills/knowledge needed

To respond imaginatively to the stimulus offered in this activity, the children need to have a varied vocabulary and be confident in its use. They should have mastered some of the skills needed to plan and review their own writing.

Key background information

This activity relies on imagination, and anything goes as far as content is concerned! Your role is as a facilitator, helping the children to explore their ideas. It is important, also, to reinforce the ideas of rhythm and cadence (intonation), so that the children's finished work not only looks like a poem on the page, but sounds rhythmic when it is read aloud.

Preparation

Make a collection of boxes, jars and other small storage containers. Try to find at least one 'special' box which will trigger the children's imagination – for example, one which is patterned, coloured, made in an unusual shape or made from an unusual material. It might even smell of spices or perfume, or look as though it has come from abroad. If possible, obtain some posters or book illustrations which have an 'other-worldly' appearance.

Resources needed

Boxes and other containers, as above, with one 'special' box; a board or flip chart; writing materials; fine white card, scissors, felt-tipped pens (see 'Suggestion(s) for support'); posters or illustrated books (see above); photocopiable page 139 (see 'Display ideas').

What to do

Spread out the collection of containers on a table in front of you. Talk with the children about the little boxes, tins and jars which almost everybody keeps at home – on the shelf, in the kitchen and so on. Discuss what can be kept in such containers: drawing pins, paper clips, buttons, elastic bands, nails and so on.

Produce the 'special' box which you have chosen as the stimulus for writing. Explore its design, and talk about what makes it special and different from the others on the table. Is it the shape, the colour, the materials? Holding the box as though it were very precious, suggest that it might contain a collection of invisible objects. If it were a 'magic box', what might it contain? Encourage the children to make suggestions along such lines as: *a box of memories, sounds, colours, wishes, dreams, nightmares.*

Use the flip chart to scribe some of the children's ideas. Take a vote (by a show of hands) on which idea they want to work on as a class, and make a preliminary list of the box's contents. For example, if 'box of sounds' is the choice, scribe a list of sounds: *birdsong, pop music, laughter, traffic, people talking* and so on. Encourage the children to be more adventurous; they may suggest *fountains, lullaby, whispering, ticking, stillness* and so on.

Now encourage the children to extend their ideas by thinking about how they might describe such sounds and/or where the sounds might be found – for example, *the sprinkling of a fountain in a garden, the whispering of the waves on a lake, the ticking of a clock in a dark bedroom, the stillness of the ice on the mountain peaks.* On the flip chart, show how these suggestions can be strung together, with each idea given two lines:

> the sprinkling of a fountain
> on a hot summer's day
> the whispering of cooling waves
> on a sandy shore
> the ticking of an ancient clock
> on the castle wall
> the stillness of the mountains
> on a frosty morning...

Now they should think of a first line for the poem, along the lines of *My box overflows with sounds* or *Music spills from my box* or *I keep sounds in my magic box...* Show the children how to work at it, until you (and they) achieve the phrase that best suits the poem.

Begin to add more ideas from the list or from new suggestions, line by line, explaining that you need to listen to the rhythms as you go along. Remind the children that you don't need to read aloud, but can 'say' the words inside your head. The class poem might begin to look like this:

Sounds

Sounds spill from my magic box:
gentle waves whispering
secrets to the shore,
tall trees singing lullabies
to the distant stars,
time ticking from a clock
on the old castle wall,
mountains making music
in the stillness of the morning...

Now take some of the children's ideas for the ending of the poem – which is often the most difficult part to write. They might suggest an ending such as:

Put back the lid
and gently close the box.
or Close the lid before
the magic drains away.

Divide the class into their groups and let each choose a kind of box to write about. Each group should choose several different ideas for the box: weathers, dreams, surprises, tastes and so on. They can write as a group or individually.

Emphasize the process of composition which you have just demonstrated, so that the children have a strategy for tackling this kind of poem when they are working independently. Remind them to:
▲ make a simple list;
▲ extend each idea;
▲ draft a poem with two lines for each idea;
▲ write appropriate opening and ending lines to 'top and tail' the poem.
Reinforce the need to listen for a beat or rhythm, cutting out or adding words as necessary. If there isn't a steady rhythm, they should still listen for 'cadence': a pattern of

stresses that flows naturally and 'sounds right'. When the children have completed their first drafts, they can read them aloud to each other; or you could act as editor, helping them to get the best out of their work.

To finish off, the children can use photocopiable page 139 to display their 'best' work inside a box-shape. (See 'Display ideas' below.)

Suggestion(s) for extension
The most able children could work on a poem derived from the 'box of dreams' idea, perhaps concentrating on the memories stored inside an old person's head:

Memories

Inside my Grandma's head
are a million memories:
the day she started school
in buckled sandals and a pale pink dress,
the day she got lost
among dark shadows and tall whispering trees,
the day she went to a party
in shiny shoes and a green frilly frock...

Suggestion(s) for support
Less confident children could try a simpler version of the magic box, such as a set of colours, tastes or smells. Ask each child to think of a smell he or she knows: 'The smell of vinegar.' *Where?* 'On my fish and chips.' He or she can write this idea as one long line, or cut it into two. Either scribe for each child or ask them to write their lines on strips of paper.

Cut out a box shape from card and paste the children's lines on it in order, with first and last lines that everyone is happy with. The result might look as shown in Figure 8:

Inside the magic box
is the smell of a rose in the garden,
of sausages sizzling in the pan,
of cakes baking in the oven,
of my dad's after-shave in the bathroom,
of my big brother's trainers in his sports bag,
of the sea on the first day
of the holidays.
I close the box, keeping everything safe
for another day.

Figure 8

Opportunities for IT

The children could work in groups, using the word processor to draft and craft their writing. Different children in the group could concentrate on particular lines, perhaps with one child (or an adult) acting as scribe.

Each completed poem could be presented inside a graphic of a box or other container, drawn using an art or drawing package.

Display ideas

Make one copy per child of photocopiable page 139 on thin card. Ask each child to cut out the two matching shapes. The child can then copy out his or her poem in 'best' writing on one shape, and use felt-tipped pens to make a lid design on the other. The 'lid' can then be attached to the box, using staples as hinges.

Reference to photocopiable sheet

The box outline on photocopiable page 139 can be used to display the children's poems. When the writing and colouring is completed, the lid should be cut out and stapled over the writing, so that the closed 'box' hides the poem.

A box for a poem

Box of

by

To use expressive language to convey serious personal thoughts and concerns. To produce and redraft poems individually.

†† *Whole class, pairs.*

🕐 *50 minutes.*

Previous skills/knowledge needed

The children should have some background knowledge of current news items or of environmental issues, and should be able to discuss their concerns. They should be familiar with the skills of drafting and editing their own written work.

Key background information

This activity is based on the idea of contrast, which is a powerful teaching tool. Imaginative work on opposites is an excellent way of encouraging children to explore issues related to the wider world – for example, looking closely at the concept of peace allows them to bring ideas about war into focus. The relatively abstract starting point of contrast allows children's thoughts and feelings about famine, loneliness, pollution or war to be explored in the safe and supportive environment of the classroom. This activity brings a personal dimension to the social studies curriculum.

Preparation

With the children's help, make a news frieze of cuttings on a current social or environmental issue from newspapers, pamphlets, posters and so on. Obtain some relevant reference materials (books, newspaper articles, photographs and so on) to help explore the theme in a wider context. Also obtain some illustrated books on gardening or parks which can be used to explore seasonal or weather contrasts (see 'Suggestion(s) for support).

Resources needed

Newspaper articles, books and photographs on war, pollution, homelessness, famine or a similar topic; illustrated books on gardening or parks; a board or flip chart; writing materials.

What to do

Gather the children in the library corner or another comfortable area where they have a clear view of the flip chart. Say that you are going to explore the idea of opposites, and ask the children for suggestions: day and night, summer and winter, black and white, high and low and so on. Scribe these ideas on the flip chart.

Now show some of the photographs and cuttings which you have collected, and look at the news frieze together. Based on these starters, brainstorm some more contrasting ideas of a deeper and possibly more emotive kind – for example, loneliness and having lots of friends, poor and rich, sad and happy, unemployed and having a good job, illness and health, famine and plenty, war and peace.

Scribe some of these opposites on the flip chart and discuss how a sharp contrast can emphasize how you feel: how warm you are if you come in out of the cold, how cold the sea feels if you have been lying in the sun, how extra-fit you feel when your flu is better, how marvellous it is to run around in the playground after sitting still in the classroom all morning, and so on. The children will have lots of experience to bring to this discussion, so take time to listen and encourage everyone to take part.

Return to the contrasting ideas on the flip chart and demonstrate how these opposites can be built into a poem. Take 'war and peace', for example. First, in discussion, highlight the idea of peace: security, tranquillity, freedom to go where we want, to enjoy holidays, to be able to sleep peacefully at night and so on. Remembering what the children may have seen on TV and in newspaper photographs, encourage them to contrast their thoughts about peace with thoughts of war: insecurity, fear, noise, being marched away from their homes, trying to sleep in tents or on the bare mountain-side, losing sight of their parents.

If the children think about 'famine and plenty', they should use a similar strategy. First discuss what 'plenty' means: not being hungry, having lots to eat (especially at parties and at Christmas), being able to choose our favourite foods and so on. Contrast that with 'famine': always feeling hungry, never having enough to eat, being forced to eat any available food whether they like it or not – no choice or preference.

Using the children's suggestions, show them how to write a contrasting poem on 'War and Peace'. First, collect sights, sounds, feelings and images of war: smoke rising like a grey ribbon, gunfire like distant thunder, shattered buildings, fear of being injured, horror of being lost, despair... Contrast these images with those of peace: wind sighing in the trees, an ice-cream van playing a happy tune, welcoming lights at home, being safely swept up in a parent's arms, hope... and so on.

Put the images together in two contrasting verses – for example:

War
Smoke rises like a ribbon
and children scream with fear.
Guns boom like distant thunder
and old women cry in despair.

Peace
The wind sighs in the trees
and a child shouts with laughter.
Home is lit with welcoming lights
and Grandma smiles with joy.

Try another example, such as 'famine and plenty'. Use the children's suggestions to generate a similar 'contrast' poem:

Famine
Empty bellies, great dark eyes,
children sob with desperate longing,
grabbing at food the flies have left.
Hunger without end.

Plenty
Full tummies, half-empty plates,
jellies, ice-cream, chocolate cake,
left-overs scraped into the bin.
Food enough and more.

Let the children work in pairs, using the list of opposites on the flip chart as a starting point to draft ideas for a poem. They should think of sights, sounds, images and feelings, as in the examples above. Between them, each pair should write a poem built on contrasts.

Children who are willing to read their poems aloud should practise with a partner. Encourage the children to vary their delivery, pace and emphasis. When some of the poems have been read aloud, discuss the way in which contrasting the horror of war with the tranquillity of peace can make a war poem more poignant. Point to a specific pair of contrasting images, such as *Empty bellies* and *Full tummies* in the 'Famine and Plenty' poem above. Look for powerful contrasts in the children's writing, and bring them to the notice of the other children.

Suggestion(s) for extension

If children (having worked with a partner) are ready to work on individual poems, suggest that they choose new titles for themselves. Through contrasting verses, the more sophisticated writers can explore quite difficult concepts, such as birth and death, then and now, freedom and captivity or youth and old age. These children can work at their own pace, creating and employing powerful images, sound patterns and so on. They might try to make contrasts in the same verse, or even line by line:

Then and now
Slender feet, fast as the wind,
slow feet, creeping like shadows.
Spine as straight as a sapling,
spine twisted like a root.
Skin smooth as pearls, unmarked,
wrinkled skin, mapped with pain.
Eyes bright and blue as sapphires,
jewelled eyes, still shining.

Encourage these confident writers to try out different structures, and to work at their poems until they are fully satisfied with the results.

Suggestion(s) for support

Those children who need support in writing poems may find it easier to work from contrasting pictures – for example, a garden (or tree, or pond) in summer and in winter. Books intended for gardeners will be useful for this purpose. The concrete image of a tree, for example, can help the child to think about seasonal contrasts:

Winter and summer
Bare black branches
reaching for a grey sky,
no birds, no leaves,
trees waiting for spring.

Branches thick and green
with leaves, blue skies,
birds singing, apples swelling,
trees ready for autumn.

It may be necessary for adult helpers to scribe for children who need support. If so, make sure that these children are given the opportunity to read their poems aloud and gain satisfaction from the completed work.

Assessment opportunities
Look out for children who can discuss and write about these sensitive themes with confidence and insight. Note how well they grasp the idea of contrast, and what vocabulary they use to express their feelings.

Opportunities for IT
Some children might use the word processor to originate their work; others might prefer to type their completed poems. The poems could be presented using a word processor – perhaps with suitable illustrations scanned from line drawings made by the children, or created using an art or drawing package. The children could experiment with different font styles, sizes and colours in order to express the idea of contrasts in the presentation of their work. The poems could be presented as a class book, using a word processor or desktop publishing package.

Display ideas
The children can copy out their poems on sheets of thin card that are folded in half, so that each contrasting verse is written on a separate facing page (see Figure 9). Each verse can be illustrated, perhaps using contrasting colours on the two pages.

Folded A4 sheet of card

Figure 9

KING AM I!

To write a fantasy poem in a free style, using rhythm but not rhyme. To use descriptive language in an imaginative context.

†† *Whole class, groups, then individual work.*

🕐 *40 minutes.*

Previous skills/knowledge needed
The children should be used to letting their imagination roam freely in creative writing. They should know that poems, like songs, often rely on rhythm to make them scan or 'sound right'. They should be able to draft and edit their own written work, and be used to sharing it with others in the class or group.

Key background information
This activity highlights the importance of rhythm in free verse. It also requires the children to imagine new worlds and to describe what they might do if they were in positions of power – not political power, but the creative power to make a fantasy scenario real. This imagined power is thus linked, in the activity, to the children's ability to visualise and describe incredible things.

Preparation
Read some poems of magic and mystery to the children. An excellent selection can be found in *The Magic Tree* edited by David Woolger (OUP 1981), and in *Otherworlds* edited by Judith Nicholls (Faber 1995). Make one copy per child of photocopiable page 140. Obtain a commercial paint catalogue or sample card, and a drum or other percussion instrument.

Resources needed
Photocopiable page 140; a board or flip chart; writing materials; a thesaurus; a commercial paint catalogue or sample card; a drum or other percussion instrument; paints, brushes, paper.

What to do
Gather the class in the library corner and read 'The paint box' by E.V. Rieu (photocopiable page 140) to them. Encourage comments on the content of the poem. 'You don't get crimson and white tigers... or blue camels and purple panthers!' is often the first reaction. Establish that this is a poem about the magic and mystery of the imagination. Highlight the language that the poet has used to create a 'magical' feel – for example, *Ivory black and emerald green...* Ask the children to repeat the first two lines together, and encourage them to listen to the rhythm.

POETRY

Ask the children to say which colours the poet has used in this poem. Suggest that they search for other exciting colour words, using the paint catalogue (or sample card) and a thesaurus. Encourage them to pick out colour words which have that indefinable 'magic sound' about them – for example: *maroon, peacock, saffron, vermilion...* Suggest that the children each note down three colour words that they like for their sound alone. List some of these on the flip chart.

Ask why the second speaker in the poem might want 'somebody utterly new' and 'a colour that nobody knows'. Encourage the children to see that the poem is about the freedom of the imagination to create new worlds.

Give out copies of 'The Paint Box' and ask the children to read it silently. Suggest that they listen to the rhythms in their heads, and underline any line whose *sound* they particularly like.

Divide the class into three groups and suggest that each group reads a verse aloud, with emphasis on the rhythm. You might use a percussion instrument to beat out the rhythm very softly behind the children's voices.

Read out the poem again and discuss the fact that it is written in the form of a dialogue between two people, but that we don't find out who they are. We must imagine their faces and their voices; we don't know whether they are men or women, boys or girls, or where this is happening. Encourage the children to visualise the people who are talking to each other. The whole poem is pure fantasy, so no-one can be wrong!

Through discussion with the children, try to tease out

who the second speaker is likely to be. What kind of person is he or she? What does he or she do? Is he or she an artist? A wizard? A king? Scribe some of the children's suggestions on the flip chart – for example, *artist, witch, magician, wizard, king, queen.*

Now ask the children what they might do if they were kings, queens or magicians for a day. How might they change ordinary, everyday things? E.V. Rieu's artist paints animals in new colours – where would the children like to start? Using some of their suggestions, write a set of titles for fantasy poems on the flip chart – for example: *King am I, Queen am I, Magician am I, Artist am I, Wizard am I, Astronaut am I, Gardener am I...*

Choose one of the titles and brainstorm some possibilities that (for example) a magic gardener might grow, remembering the range of colours used in 'The Paint Box'. Arrange the suggestions into a rhythmic poem, such as:

apples in indigo, peacock, hyacinth
buttercups in lavender, violet, puce
grass in ebony, coal-black, jet
pears in silver, copper, gold
daisies in crimson, scarlet, vermilion...

Read the poem aloud and listen for the rhythm of each line. Does the first line (in this example) work? Perhaps it would sound better if it were altered to *apples in peacock, indigo, mauve...* The last word in the line certainly needs to be a one-beat (if not one-syllable) word. (*Vermilion* in the last line works because it only has one stress or beat, though it has more than one syllable.) Encourage the children to read the first line aloud, to listen and to join in the search for a satisfactory answer to the rhythm problem.

When the children are happy with the sound of the poem and with the magical flowers and fruit that the gardener might grow, ask them to work individually, choosing one of the other suggested titles (or making one up) and brainstorming some outlandish ideas, changing colours, textures, shapes, movements – even reasons! Remind the children that, although the poem doesn't need to rhyme, its rhythm is very important.

When the children have each made a word-web or list, get them to use their ideas in a draft poem. The poem should start with the line *King am I* (or *Astronaut am I, Artist am I, Poet am I,* and so on). Then they should construct a fantasy poem, imagining what they would do if they were a king, queen, wizard or extraterrestrial creature with the power to alter people's lives. Emphasize that going to Disneyland or winning the lottery jackpot does *not* have that touch of magic that you are looking for.

Remind the children that, unlike E.V. Rieu, they are not making up a rhyming poem. Help them observe that pop music and advertising jingles are very rhythmic, even when they don't rhyme. Suggest that they read through their

'Gardener am I,
   magic trees weighed down
   with apples painted
   forget-me-not-blue.
I wave my silver hoe
and a million daisies grow,
   their ruby faces
   turned towards the sun.
I dig deep for you,
find potatoes shining
   like nuggets of gold,
I climb high for you,
pick fat silvery pears,
   marbled cherries, peaches
   dipped in ultramarine.
      Gardener am I!'

poem carefully, adjusting it until they are happy with the rhythm or beat. The finished poem might look like the example shown on page 75.

Encourage the children to remember the element of magic – the unexpected phrases – while always keeping in mind that the rhythm helps to give the poem its power.

Suggestion(s) for extension

More confident children could go on to write a poem in the form of a dialogue, as E.V. Rieu has done. Remind them to read through their lines, changing or exchanging words until they arrive at a satisfactory beat. The following example has a complex rhythmic pattern:

'King am I. What shall I do
to please you best, my dear?
Shall I paint the sky bright green,
or gild the rolling waves?'

'Queen am I. For my delight
build me a silver boat,
so I can sail across the skies
to a land that no-one knows.'

Children could work in pairs on this poem, each taking a role and reading out lines of dialogue, using the sound to help them redraft the poem until it flows smoothly.

Suggestion(s) for support

If the children are unhappy with this kind of open-ended imaginative task, arrange for them to work with a sympathetic and more confident partner. They could look at the poem by E.V. Reiu and rewrite it, changing the colours and turning 'paint' into 'write' – for example:

'Gentian, mauve and turquoise blue,
Orange and lime and cyclamen red –
What shall I write to give pleasure to you?'
'Write me a poem that's utterly true.'

... and so on. This verse follows the rhythmic pattern of the original (it also rhymes, but it doesn't need to do so).

Assessment opportunities

Note those children who have an affinity for rhythm – who can listen to the beat of their lines and see how to alter the words to bring out the underlying rhythms of the poem.

Note those children who can work in the imaginative way that the activity demands, without being frightened off by the freedom it offers.

Opportunities for IT

This is an ideal activity for children to experiment with an art package in order to create a picture of their magical world. They will need to be able to select colours from the palette – perhaps using the mixing option to create their own colours, or using a screen mode which has multiple colours. The pictures could then be used as backgrounds for the children's poems. The picture could be imported into a word processor or desktop publishing package, and the poem either written into the white spaces of the picture or superimposed on the picture (using it as a background).

Display ideas

The children can make a 'magic garden' or 'magic mountain' display to show their fantasy poems to best effect. They could stick the poems onto pieces of gold or silver backing paper, then paste them onto a dark red backing sheet filled with tree shapes in foil paper. They could make leaves and fruit that look like jewels, using beads, sequins or scraps of silver foil. The foreground could be filled with flower shapes in silver and gold. Encourage the children to work together, creating a shared vision of something marvellous and 'utterly new'.

Reference to photocopiable sheet

The poem on photocopiable page 140 is a surreal and challenging stimulus for the children's imaginative poems.

Using a Pattern

Using a pattern for a poem allows children to try out different strategies and techniques within a basic framework. This gives them confidence and makes them less inhibited about putting the first words down on paper. The old cliché about the futility of reinventing the wheel can be applied to poetry: we can encourage children to use patterns and structures developed by other poets. Far from inhibiting creativity, this approach often releases language and ideas – especially among those who need support in writing poetry.

If children are aware that the first line in each verse of a poem should begin *The moon is like...*, they know how to start and can focus on the image which follows. This works best if they have made a list of possible comparisons before they start on their first draft. They can then pick out an interesting simile (such as *The moon is like a silver boat...*) to create the first line. For the second line, they could think about what boats do (*sailing, floating, rocking*) and where this happens, bearing in mind that they are describing night: *sailing on dark deep waves*. The pattern is easy to follow, but it leads to the satisfaction of creating an original poem.

It is worth encouraging more adventurous writers to move on and to experiment within new formats. However, they should still try to fit their words to the pattern they have chosen. Children can also think of new variations on a pattern. Sequence is a good example of this. Most children will start by working on the sequence of days in the week or months in the year. However, if given free rein, they may suggest unexpected sequences: from raindrops to the ocean, or from a tree to the paper they are using.

Some children find it helpful to hang their poems on a published poet's pattern. An appropriate poem can both provide a starting point and open up exciting creative possibilities. Let the children share and exchange ideas, stand patterns on their heads and turn them inside-out. The results will surprise and excite you.

POETRY

THROUGH THAT DOOR

To listen for and discuss rhyme. To write a descriptive poem based on the rhyme scheme of a published poem.

†† *Whole class or group (at least six), then individual work.*

🕐 *45 minutes.*

Previous skills/knowledge needed

The children should have experience of listening and responding as a group, listing or brainstorming their ideas for a poem, and drafting their work. They should be able to imagine what a desert island might look like, and be able to project into a fantasy world. The ability to use a rhyming dictionary would be useful.

Key background information

This activity, which can be used with similar rhyming poems such as 'A song of sevens' by Irene Rawnsley (in *A Blue Poetry Paintbox* edited by John Foster, OUP 1994), expands the children's sense of imaginative possibilites and shows them how to build a poem using a listing technique. It also encourages them to develop their listening skills.

Preparation

Make one copy per child of photocopiable page 141. Obtain a rhyming dictionary such as *Walker's Rhyming Dictionary of the English Language* by Michael Freeman, RKP, 1985.

Resources needed

Photocopiable page 141; writing materials, felt-tipped pens; a board or flip chart; a rhyming dictionary.

What to do

Make sure that the children are sitting without distractions, ready to participate in a listening session. Read aloud John Cotton's poem 'Through that door' (photocopiable page 141). At the end of the reading, leave a 'thinking space' of a minute or so, then ask the children to consider whether or not this poem rhymes. Read out the first verse again, suggesting that they concentrate on the rhyming words: *Wall/tall* and *you/knew*. Ask for some more rhyming words which the poet could have used – for example, *ball, call, fall, small, sprawl... few, flew, stew, blue...*

Working orally, explore ways in which some of the new rhyming words might have been incorporated into the poem – for example:

Through that door	Through that door
Is a garden with a wall,	Is a garden with a wall,
Autumn colours burning	Where primroses grow
As leaves begin to fall.	And songbirds call.

This work will help to establish in the children's minds that a poet writing a rhyming poem has the difficult task of keeping two ideas going at the same time: to find a set of words that rhyme, and to choose words that make sense. It's no good finding a splendid rhyme which, whatever you do, simply won't fit into the sense of the poem.

The children could develop this part of the activity by working with a rhyming dictionary, looking for new rhymes and trying to fit them into the poem.

This leads on to using the rhyming pattern of 'Through that door' to create a new poem. Ask the children to think how a closed door is used: for security, warmth, keeping people apart from one another and so on. Now explore the idea of an open door: how it might lead into a different room, to the outside world and so on.

Ask the children to listen to John Cotton's poem again, suggesting that they try to think of ways to describe the door in the poem. Settle them and read 'Through that door' once more. After the usual thinking space, ask for words

to describe the door in John Cotton's poem – for example, *The mystery door, The magic door, The door into fantasy...*

List the places on the other side of 'that door': a peaceful garden; a great ocean; a secret room; mountains, moors, rivers and forests; and a city. But this is no ordinary city: it is *the city of the mind / Where you can imagine / What you'll find.* Explore what is meant by 'the city of the mind'. Ask the children: *Is this a real city? Is it the same for everyone? What might be in **your** city of the mind?*

Give out the copies of page 141 and let the children read through them, underlining lines they particularly like in red felt-tipped pen, mysterious words in blue, ideas they would like to question in green, and so on. Encourage them to discuss their findings with each other (working in groups or as a whole class).

Now suggest that the children go on to write about their own 'magic doors' and some of the things and places they might find on the other side. Ask for suggestions, and scribe some of their ideas on the flip chart in list form. The children might suggest a treasure island, a haunted castle, an underwater funfair, a moonscape... and so on.

Take one idea and, with the children's help, expand it into a list of three things on the flip chart. For example, the list for *a desert island* might read:

a sunken ship
a treasure chest
a tall palm tree

For *a haunted house*, the three things might be:

a cobwebbed attic
a threadbare curtain
a deep dark cellar

Using *Through that door* as an opening line, assemble some of the ideas on the flip chart to make up a new poem. Explain to the children that you do not intend to make the poem rhyme at this stage, since it is difficult to write a good rhyming poem. You might produce something like this:

Through that door
Is a desert island
Where a sunken ship
Rolls under the waves;
Where a treasure chest,
Locked and bolted, lies
Half-hidden in the sand
Under a tall palm tree.

Now show the children how they might go about writing a rhyming poem like one of the verses in 'Through that door' – for example:

Through that door
Ghosts lie in wait
In a haunted castle
With a high spiked gate.
A threadbare curtain
Flaps in the air,
And up from the cellar
Black spiders stare.

Discuss some possible alternatives to the last two lines:

And a sound of footsteps   *or*   But don't look in the attic
On the crumbling stair.   Black bats roost there.

Now suggest that the children make their own poems. They should take a different magical location for each verse, expand it by making a list as above, then set it in lines. They can use rhymes or not, as they prefer.

Help the children to work from their draft poems to finished pieces. Take time to ask questions, help with editing and listen to the rhythms of the piece, until each child is satisfied with what he or she has written.

Suggestion(s) for extension

More able children could try to find new rhyming words for other verses of John Cotton's poem – for example:

Through that door
Is the great ocean-sea
With high grey waves
Rolling wild and free.

Alternatively, they could write a different first line to make a completely new poem: *Over that mountain, Across that river, Down that tunnel* and so on.

Suggestion(s) for support

Children who have difficulty in writing a poem could concentrate on writing one new verse only, working almost entirely from a simple list – for example, a garden with roses, birds, trees, grass:

Through that door
Is a summer garden
With roses and birds
And grass and trees.

Assessment opportunities

Note (by listening) those children who readily grasp the idea that if a rhyming poem is to work, the rhyming words must not only rhyme successfully but also make sense. Note those children who can use words to create a fantasy landscape, finding ideas which fit the magic location they have chosen.

Opportunities for IT

The children could use a word processor to draft their poems. They may need to save their first draft and then retrieve it later for further work. The teacher could also provide a starter file, with lines of the poem already entered in the word processor for the children to work on.

The children could also use an art or drawing package to design a door and present the completed poem behind it. The picture of the doorway, including the door and door frame, should be created first. This file should be printed out, and then the door should be erased from the picture. The poem should then be typed into the door frame, and its font style or size adjusted so that it fits the frame. This framed poem should be printed out, so that it can be placed behind the original door printout. Each step of the work should be saved to disk separately, so that it can be retrieved if necessary.

Display ideas

These poems naturally lend themselves to being written inside an opening door, gate or window. Ask the children each to write out their poem in 'best' down the middle of a sheet of plain A4 paper (using line guides for writing, if necessary). They should then cover the poem with another plain sheet on which they have drawn a door wide and tall enough to accommodate the writing. (It is best to check this by holding it up to a sunny window, if possible.) Finally, they should cut down the picture so that the door can be

Figure 1

opened to reveal the poem, and then paste the edges of the picture sheet over the poem sheet. (See Figure 1.)

These 'opening door' poems can also be made into a class display by painting a long garden wall (showing bricks or stones) and gluing the 'doors' in a sequence along the wall, so that they can be opened up to reveal the poems.

Reference to photocopiable sheet

Photocopiable page 141 presents a rhymed poem in verses, each verse starting with the same line. The children can use this pattern to create their own similar poems (or single verses).

IF I WERE AN ARTIST

To use the pattern of form and content in a published poem as a basis for imaginative writing.

†† *Whole-class introduction, then individual work.*

🕘 *60 minutes.*

Previous skills/knowledge needed

The children should be familiar with the skills of drafting and editing. They should be able to follow the pattern of a poem, recognizing how the form and content of a poem like 'Portrait of a dragon' are structured and using it as a template. In addition, they need to know the names and characteristics of some mythical beasts such as dragons, unicorns, griffins and so on. They should have an understanding that such creatures did not exist in reality, but that they live on in the world of legend.

Key background knowledge

This activity provides a pattern for designing a dragon, using words, to the poet's individual specification. Of course, no-one has ever seen a dragon; so the poem encourages the reader or listener to enter a world of imagination in company with the poet. You can encourage this use of fantasy by exploring ancient and modern myths and legends with the children, so that they become familiar with such imaginary creatures as Pegasus, Medusa, hobbits, goblins, elves, shoggoths, unicorns and so on.

Preparation

Find some illustrated books or posters showing mythical or fantastic beasts – for example, *Dragon Poems* by John Foster (OUP, 1991) or *Fabulous Beasts* by Monika Beisner and Alison Lurie (Jonathan Cape, 1981). Find a picture of a unicorn (for example, there is one in *Fabulous Beasts*; unicorn posters are also available). Make copies (one of each per child) of photocopiable pages 142 and 143.

Resources needed

Photocopiable pages 142 and 143; books or posters showing mythical creatures, including a picture of a unicorn; a board or flip chart; writing materials; A4 blank paper, line guides, adhesive, silver glitter; black card or sugar paper.

What to do

Read 'Portrait of a Dragon' (photocopiable page 142) to the class. Establish the fact that a dragon is a mythical creature: no-one has ever met one! This means, of course, that the poet's images of a dragon are not tied to reality in the way that *the greyness of an elephant* or *the stripiness of a tiger* would be. However, a mythical beast can still be described using colours and shapes borrowed from the world.

By asking questions, find out whether the children

remember how the poet built up her picture of the dragon: a silver river for its tail, blue mountains for its back and so on. Give out copies of photocopiable page 142 and ask the children to read the poem silently. Now ask them to imagine alternatives – for example, pyramids or rooftops for the back; church spires or park railings for the spikes; a python or a roller-coaster to make the tail. Encourage them to think of 'way-out' designs, varying and combining shapes. Help them to expand their imaginative horizons, so that each answer builds on the one before; and make it clear that all ideas are welcome if the children can explain their choices.

Look closely at the poster or picture of a unicorn. Like a dragon, a unicorn is a mythical beast: no-one has ever seen one. Suggest that if we were artists, we could 'copycat' the poem 'Portrait of a dragon' to design a unicorn. Ask them what would make a good head, eyes, body, hooves, tail and so on. Elicit their ideas through 'word-trading' (see 'Introduction', page 5). Ask them to make a list of ideas (in their drafting books, if they have these) under headings such as *Eyes*, *Body* and *Tail*.

On the flip chart, scribe the opening lines of the poem, substituting *unicorn* for *dragon*:

If I were an artist
I'd paint the portrait
of a unicorn.

Suggest that the children begin their own draft poems in the same way. (If some children have other ideas, let them work independently.) Go on to explain how to copy the structure of other verses from the poem – for example:

For his body I'd borrow a horse as white as milk.	For his eyes I'd use diamonds sparkling like stars.

His tail would be a waterfall, silver in the moonlight.	For his horn I'd need an icicle, cold as winter.

Build up the poem, scribing the first line of each new stanza on the flip chart and encouraging the children to go ahead with their own ideas, at their own pace. Once the children have drafted their own versions, they should use copies of photocopiable page 143 to write out their 'Portrait of a unicorn' poems.

Ask the children to think of an ending which echoes the magical element of the original poem – perhaps by collecting together a set of synonyms or images for *white* or *silver*. Scribe a list of ideas on the board and encourage the children to work some of them into a rhythmic chant, such as:

I'd use all white and silver – ivory, marble, frost and snow,	daisies, lilies, snowdrops, and the sparkle from a thousand stars.

Discuss the finished drafts and help to correct spelling errors. The children should use line guides to write out their poems in 'best' on blank A4 paper. Then they can put a little adhesive around the edges of the finished poem, sprinkle the page with silver glitter, allow to dry and shake off the excess. The unicorn poems can then be mounted on black card or sugar paper.

Suggestion(s) for extension
More confident writers could use the structure of 'Portrait of a dragon' to write poems on other mythical or fantastic creatures which appeal to them.

Suggestion(s) for support
Less confident children could be helped to construct a few verses, using two lines per verse and keeping the language simple – for example:

For his head I'd use a silver balloon.	For his hooves I'd use ten-pence pieces.

Assessment opportunities
Note those children who can go beyond their everyday vocabulary and experiment with a range of exciting ideas. Look for those who can follow the suggested pattern, but also give it their own individual touch. Note those who have difficulty in accommodating to a mythical context, and whose choice of words remains confined by everyday reality.

Opportunities for IT
Some children could use a word processor to draft their poems. The final presented poem could be formatted with different colours or text fonts and styles to make it more

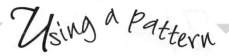

interesting. Children could also use an art package to draw a picture of their dragon; if the text is added to the picture on screen, different verses could be positioned in the spaces around the dragon.

Display ideas

For a 'magical' effect, suggest that some of the children copy out their work in silver pen on black paper, then pin the poem to a silver backing sheet and edge it with strands of tinsel.

Reference to photocopiable sheets

The dragon poem on photocopiable page 142 should be read by the children and used as a model for their unicorn poems. The writing frame on photocopiable page 143 should be used by the children to present their unicorn poems in 'best' after they have drafted and polished them in rough form.

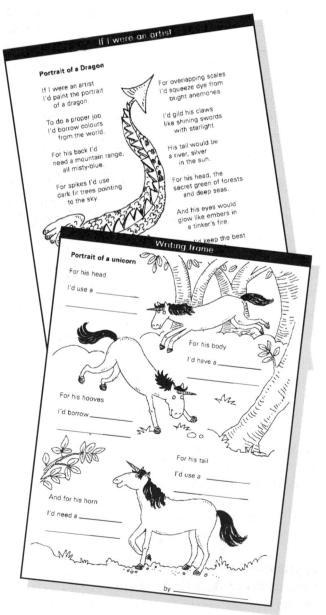

ABOVE AND BEYOND

To use a range of different prepositions as a basis for a descriptive and imaginative poem.

†† *Whole class, then individual work.*

🕐 *30 minutes.*

Previous skills/knowledge needed

The children should be able to use a varied vocabulary with confidence, including prepositions such as *beside, beyond* and *above*.

Key background information

This activity requires the children to think and write about different places. They will need to visualize and describe what might occupy the spaces surrounding their homes, either in reality or in imagination. This activity could easily become part of a topic on the built environment.

Preparation

It might be useful to collect some exterior photographs of places where the children live (houses, flats, gardens, balconies and so on), perhaps mounting them for a classroom display. Ask the children to find books about houses and homes in the school or classroom library. If there are any underground workings in the local area, it might be of interest to pinpoint these and to find out something of their history. Books about underground creatures would also be useful. Make one copy per child of photocopiable page 144, and some copies of photocopiable page 145 (see 'Suggestion(s) for support').

Resources needed

Photocopiable pages 144 and 145; books (or other information sources) on the local environment, underground creatures and houses and homes; a board or flip chart; writing materials.

What to do

Gather the class together and invite them to suggest words which are used to describe where things are. Start by pointing upwards and asking the children to describe the space 'up there' above your head. Encourage the use of prepositions: *above/over your head*. How about the space around you? The space underneath your feet? and so on.

Say that these useful space or position words are known as **prepositions**. From the children's suggestions, make a collection of such words on the flip chart. Draw a house in the middle of the chart and surround it with suitably-placed prepositions: *above, over, below, beneath, under, around, beside, beyond* and so on.

Tell the children that you are going to read them a poem about a house, and that this poem uses a different preposition at the start of each verse. On the flip chart, blitz some of the things that might be above the house (birds, sky, clouds), around the house (trees, grass, wind), beneath the house and so on. In particular, discuss with the children what things might lie below the house: old mine workings, underground tunnels, creatures that live underground, tree roots that take up water from the soil, and so on. Use descriptions or pictures from books to point out useful ideas.

Read out 'Beyond my house' (photocopiable page 144) and talk about its content, commenting on the pattern of the poem. Point out that each verse begins with a line of the form: *[Preposition] my house.* Go back to the drawing of the house and the prepositions that you brainstormed earlier, and look for other prepositions that the poet might have used, such as *through, beneath, outside* and so on.

Suggest that the children draft their own poems about a house, using an outline sketch like the one on the flip chart as a starting point. They should gather together a set of ideas for each space: above the house, below it, beside it... When they have compiled enough ideas, the children should begin to draft the poem. The first line of each verse should be *[Preposition] my/our house*, and the following lines should use three or four appropriate ideas from the sketch. (If they prefer, they can invent their own pattern for the poem – as long as they include a preposition somewhere in each verse.)

When the children have finished, help them to edit their drafts.

Suggestion(s) for extension

Children who finish early could go on to write new poems using a similar pattern, with a different preposition in each stanza. For example, they might think of a different building:

The castle

Above the old castle
are flags of all the nations
flying like tethered birds,
their wings tattered scraps
of colour.

Around the old castle
is a deep dark moat,
its waters reflecting secrets
from its deep dark
history.

The children could try a variety of buildings: the haunted house, the mosque, the supermarket and so on. They could go on to write poems about the sea, mountains, the forest or the street, again concentrating on the preposition at the beginning of each stanza:

Our street

Along our street
cars are parked end to end,
their windscreens
glittering like mirrors
in the sun.

Down our street
traffic wardens roam
like hungry predators,
notebooks opened wide as
snapping jaws.

Suggestion(s) for support

Children who are struggling with the concept of prepositions might find it easier to use three prepositions only – for example, *above, beside* and *below*, as in the writing frame on photocopiable page 145. Those who lack confidence in independent writing could use this writing frame to fill in their words and phrases from the sketch outline of a house. Encourage them to keep the poem simple, but to make every effort to complete it. The finished piece might look something like this:

Above my house
is the blue sky,
birds singing and
a cloud floating along.

Beside my house
is a holly tree
with berries and
a wall to grow ivy on.

Below my house
is the earth
with spiders and
worms wriggling about.

Either ask an adult helper to read these poems aloud or encourage the children to do this for themselves. This will boost their confidence in their own ability as poets.

Assessment opportunities

Note those children who can find and use appropriate prepositions in order to write a poem about a place, relating their visual sense of space to appropriate vocabulary. Look for those who are able to follow a pattern, then extend and alter it to suit their own ideas.

Opportunities for IT

An interesting display could be created around a picture of a house, or other building, in the middle of a computer screen. The picture could be scanned from a photograph (or from the child's own line drawing), taken from a clip art collection or drawn using an art or drawing package. Once the children have placed the picture into the word processor or desktop publishing package, they can resize it and position it in the middle of the page. The verses of the poem can then be positioned around the picture.

Display ideas

The children can make pictorial frames for their poems, as follows:

1. Copy out the poem in the middle of a blank A4 sheet, using line guides (if necessary) to keep the writing straight.
2. Cover the poem with a second blank A4 sheet and fasten it in place with paper clips.
3. Hold the poem up against a sunny window (if possible) and roughly mark the outline shape of the poem with a pencil line, so that the outer edge of the top sheet becomes a frame for the poem. (See Figure 2.)
4. Use felt-tipped pens to decorate the frame by drawing birds and clouds above the house; flowers and trees beside it; worms, beetles and tree roots beneath it; and so on, as appropriate to the words of the poem.
5. Cut around the pencil line on the top sheet (using pointed scissors) to leave a hole, so that the poem shows through. Carefully stick the frame down onto the bottom sheet.
6. The framed poems can be arranged on a background frieze.

Reference to photocopiable sheets

The poem on photocopiable page 144 should be used as a stimulus for the children to write similar poems: they need to identify the basic pattern or structure of the poem, then copy and adapt this pattern for their own purposes. Photocopiable page 145 is a simple writing frame, reproducing the pattern which the children have to follow; children who have difficulty in writing their own poems may find this sheet helpful (see 'Suggestion(s) for support').

Figure 2

INSIDE MY HEAD

To write an imaginative poem using a published poem as a model. To develop awareness of the evocative qualities of a published poem. To produce a polished final poem through drafting and revising.

†† *Whole class, then individual work.*

🕐 *40 minutes.*

Previous skills/knowledge needed

The children should be used to listening to poems. They should be able to read and appreciate a piece of imaginative writing, and should have a wide vocabulary. They should be skilled in drafting and editing their own written work.

Key background information

This activity relies on the children's ability to appreciate the evocative power of Judith Nicholls' poem 'Night' and use it as a pattern for their own work. Like several other activities in this book, it requires the children to make an 'imaginative leap'. They need to describe new worlds which might exist 'inside their heads' alongside the poet's 'dark, dark wood'. It is important to explore the structure of the poem with the children, so that they can build on it. They should also examine the way that rhyme is used in the poem, though they do not need to use rhyme in their own versions.

Preparation
Find a selection of 'other-worldly' posters and children's picture books – for example, ones illustrated by Brian Wildsmith, Charles Keeping, Kozo Kakimoto, Josef Palecek, Tove Jansson and so on. Make one copy per child of photocopiable page 146.

Resources needed
Photocopiable page 146; a board or flip chart; writing materials.

What to do
Assemble the children in a comfortable space where everyone can see and hear you. Read out the poem 'Night' (photocopiable page 146), and leave a minute or two of thinking time before you ask the children to comment on the poem. Ask questions such as:
▲ *Are any lines repeated through the poem?*
▲ There's a dark dark wood / inside my head. *What does the poet mean by this?*
▲ *Listen to the first verse again. Where does the reality end and the fantasy begin?*
▲ *What does the poet mean by saying that* night has eyes*?*
▲ *How does the second verse use the sense of touch to create a 'spooky' feel?*
▲ *What picture can you see in your head when you hear the last verse? What other creatures and plants might the poet have suggested?*
▲ *How does the language used by the poet evoke a night scene?*

Give out individual copies of 'Night' and ask the children to read it silently. Can they find rhyming words? For example, the first verse has *cries/eyes* and *feet/meet*. If the children work through the poem again, they will see that there is no regular pattern of rhyme, but that each verse has at least two rhymes embedded within it.

Ask the children whether they can suggest where the action of this poem takes place. They may say: *In the mind, in the imagination, in the memory.* Examine these ideas, encouraging them to close their eyes and to create *a dark, dark wood / inside their heads.* Work through the senses, asking the children to talk about what they might hear, see, feel and smell.

Use the flip chart to scribe a web of ideas. Print the words *A dark, dark wood* in the centre of the web, with four spokes marked *Sight, Sound, Smell* and *Touch*. Gather the children's ideas in each section. Suggestions might include:
▲ **sound –** the sigh of an owl's wings, the crackle of twigs;
▲ **sight –** the cradle of the moon, the scatter of stars;

▲ **touch –** the roughness of tree trunks, the stickiness of a spider's web;
▲ **smell –** the fresh scent of rain, the musty smell of fallen leaves.

Try to get as many of the children involved in this process as you can. Encourage them to develop the simple into the complex – for example, to go from *an owl flying* to *an owl swooping overhead* to *the soft breath of an owl's wings...*

Following the pattern of 'Night', show the children how some of these ideas could be put together – for example:

There's a deep, deep wood
inside my head
where twigs crackle underfoot
and an owl's wings sigh;
where the moon rocks
in his cradle
and a scatter of stars
lights up the sky.

Let the children work as a class, making up another verse or two with you on the flip chart. Remind them that they can add different ideas of their own as they go along, and that they don't need to cram all of the suggestions on the list into the poem. Let the poem flow as the mood takes the children. They can work in groups if they prefer.

When the process of creating a poem on the flip chart

has been thoroughly explored, suggest that the children move on to a different imaginative scenario 'inside their heads' – for example:

▲ *There's a wide blue ocean*
  inside my head...
▲ *There's a deep dark cave*
  inside my head...
▲ *There's a spooky old castle*
  inside my head...
▲ *There's a far-away space station*
  inside my head...

When you have collected a number of possible scenarios on the flip chart, suggest that each child chooses one on which he or she would like to work. Some children might prefer to work on their own individual ideas – if so, this should be encouraged.

Ask the children to brainstorm an 'ideas web' appropriate to their own choice of poem, perhaps using the senses as starting points. Next, they should work some of these ideas into a first draft of a short poem, following the pattern of one of Judith Nicholls' verses. The result might look something like this:

> There's a wide blue ocean
> inside my head
> where sails whisper to the wind,
> where dolphins dance through silver spray
> and fish fly like rainbow birds,
> where waves sparkle under the sun
> and seaweed smells of salty light
> in the heat of a gilded day.

The finished poem should have approximately eight lines, some beginning with the word *where* or *and*; but there are no strict rules. The poem should feel slightly other-worldly, full of the magic of colour and sound. The children are trying to emulate the style and feeling of the original, rather than follow a rigid structure.

Help the children to edit their work, encouraging them to sift out words and phrases they don't really need. Remind them that **every word must work for its place in a poem**. Help them to look for unusual or exciting rhymes which help to stress the meaning, rather than twisting the words around to accommodate the first rhyme they think of! Finally, help them to listen for the rhythm of the lines. In this way, they develop the skill of reworking a piece until the finished version satisfies them and they feel that it is the best they can do.

Finally, the children should use line guides to copy the poem out in 'best', keeping to the middle of an A4 page with enough space surrounding the poem to make a frame. (See 'Display ideas' below.)

Suggestion(s) for extension
The most able writers could work on a poem entitled 'Inside a girl's head' or 'Inside a boy's head', emphasizing the imaginative content and perhaps focusing on the differences in attitude between boys and girls – if any! The following is an example:

> Inside a boy's head
> there is a moon rocket,
> an astronaut in a silver spacesuit,
> the smell of summer dust
> and the sharp taste of blackberries;
> and there is the Milky Way
> stretching to infinity,
> a thousand glittering stars
> but no map to show the way home –
> just a million jostling memories.

Here a set of loosely related items (which mostly have to do with space travel) are arranged in a short poem, as if they were boxed inside a boy's head. Note the inclusion of different senses: smell, taste and vision.

Suggestion(s) for support

With children who have difficulty in drafting their own poems, work on a group poem using the starter ideas already on the flip chart. Suggest that they put together ideas from the senses in two successive lines, for example: *Where I hear an owl flying / and twigs crackling.* Encourage them to add some new ideas of their own – these can easily be accommodated. The result might look something like this:

> There's a deep, deep wood
> inside my head,
> where I hear an owl flying
> and twigs crackling,
> where I can feel a sticky cobweb
> and the rough bark of a tree,
> where I can see the moon
> and a sprinkling of stars,
> all inside my head.

Assessment opportunities

Note those children who can make the 'imaginative leap', and whose work is not restrained by the facts of everyday living. Look for those who can use a range of creative vocabulary with confidence. Note those children who have difficulty in imagining beyond mundane reality.

Look for those children who can use the editing process to make the best of their work, orchestrating the combined effects of meaning, imagery and rhythm. Look for those who can also use the editing process to check for spelling and punctuation.

Opportunities for IT

You could use the word processor to set up a simple writing frame for the children to use, following the pattern of Judith Nicholls' poem. This frame should be saved to disk, so that the children can use it at different times to start their own writing. They should, of course, be encouraged to alter the frame to suit their own ideas. The starting frame might read as follows:

There's a
Inside my head
Where
Where
And
Where
And
And

This approach will reduce some of the typing needed, and will also provide a structure for the children to work with.

The completed poems could be presented inside a head shape; this could be drawn using an art or drawing package, scanned from a line drawing or taken from a clip art collection.

Display ideas

The children can make frames for their completed poems, as follows:

1. Use line guides to copy out the poem carefully in the middle of an A4 sheet, leaving a 'frame'.
2. Cover the poem with a second sheet of A4 paper (or thin A4 card) and fix the sheets together with paper clips.
3. Hold both sheets up against a sunny window (if possible) and outline the shape of the poem on the top sheet, keeping the outline irregular.
4. Decorate the frame appropriately: underwater for a 'deep, deep ocean' poem, a forest scene for a 'dark, dark wood' poem and so on.
5. Cut out the middle of the frame, so that the poem will show through the hole. Paste the frame over the poem.

A set of framed poems can be displayed on dark frieze paper.

Reference to photocopiable sheet

The poem on photocopiable page 146 can be used as a stimulus for children to write their own 'In my head' poems which echo the structure, style and atmosphere of the original.

RECIPE FOR SUMMER

To write a poem within the framework of a recipe.
To use descriptive language, including similes.
†† *Whole-class introduction, then individual work.*
🕐 *60 minutes.*

Previous skills/knowledge needed
The children should have been involved in a baking activity. It will be particularly helpful if they have followed a recipe for cakes or biscuits, so that they know how such a recipe is structured. It will also be helpful for the children to understand some common terms used in baking, such as *add, blend, whisk* and *mix.* The children should be familiar with the task of drafting and editing their written work.

Key background information
Following a given structure gives children the confidence to work on a descriptive poem, and helps them to concentrate on the 'nuts and bolts' of writing. This activity allows them to explore similes and images within the safety of a set pattern: a poem based on the recipe form with a pattern of three lines in each verse, the last line beginning with the word 'and'.

Preparation
Ask the children to bring in recipe books, or collect several examples from the school library shelves. Bring in some kitchen implements, such as a whisk, baking spoon and rolling pin. You might also wish to provide some ingredients for baking a cake: flour, eggs, sugar and so on. Make some copies of photocopiable page 147 (see 'Suggestion(s) for support' below).

Resources needed
A number of recipe books; some kitchen implements; cake ingredients (optional); a board or flip chart; writing materials, blank A4 paper, line guides; dictionaries; felt-tipped pens, scissors, adhesive.

What to do
Start this activity with a 'question and answer' session, trying to involve as many of the children as possible.

With the children grouped in front of you, ask what you might need if you were going to bake a cake. They may suggest flour, sugar, currants, butter and so on. (Show any ingredients you have brought in.) Ask them: *What are these things known as together?* Elicit the response: *The ingredients.* Now find out from the children what they would do with their ingredients: mix, whisk, blend and so on. *What tools would be needed?* Display a few kitchen implements and establish how they are used.

Look at some recipe books together, emphasizing the characteristic structure and style of a recipe. Tell the children that together you are going to write out a recipe – not for a cake, but for summer. Ask them to suggest the ingredients which would make up a perfect summer's day, starting with the weather: a clear blue sky, bright sunshine, a cool breeze and so on. Write two of these ideas on the flip chart under the heading *Weather.*

Next, gather ideas for flowers and plants – for example, red roses, scarlet geraniums, orange marigolds, honeysuckle and so on. Choose two ideas to put under the heading *Flowers.* Now encourage the children to think of insects and other creatures which they are likely to see on a summer's day, such as butterflies, bees, dragonflies, swallows, lizards and so on. Again, choose two ideas to write under the heading *Creatures.*

Now ask the children to make their own 'shopping lists' under the headings *Weather, Flowers* and *Creatures* (using drafting books, if they have these). They should write down three ideas in each list – they are allowed to 'borrow' one idea for each list from the board, but they must think of the other two themselves. When they have finished their lists, say that you will tell them how their ideas can be used to make a recipe poem.

Write the title 'Recipe for summer' on the board. Tell the children that they are ready to gather together all the ingredients which make up summer. Start with the word *Take* and write three short lines – for example:

Recipe for summer
Take a clear blue sky,
the shining sun
and a cool breeze.

With the children's help, develop each line so that it is extended into a simile or has some added description:

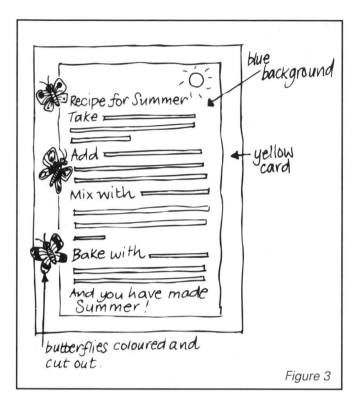

Figure 3

Take a clear blue cloudless sky,
the sun shining like a golden balloon
and a breeze as cool as mountain water.

Encourage the children to draft their own first three lines. The first line must start with the word *Take*, and each new ingredient should be on a new line.

Now model a second verse. This can follow the same pattern; but remembering that you are writing a recipe poem, start this verse with the word *Add*. The second verse might look like this:

Add red roses growing by the garden wall,
some sweet-smelling honeysuckle
and marigolds scattered like fallen stars.

Allow the children time to draft their own second verse. The third verse should also use three lines, each describing a bird or an insect. Invite the children to suggest a recipe instruction such as *Mix, whisk, blend* or *stir in*:

Mix with rainbow butterflies,
swallows swooping like arrows
and dragonflies hovering over the pond.

Again, allow the children time to draft their own verse. Complete the poem with a final verse, such as:

Bake in the yellow heat of afternoon
for three glittering months
and you have made SUMMER!

Encourage the children to write their own endings. Point out that the last line of each verse, in your example, starts with the word 'and'.

Encourage the children to polish their work. Help them to listen to the rhythms of their poems, perhaps offering redrafting suggestions. Ask them to check their spelling with a dictionary (or with the help of a partner).

Now ask the children to write out their poems in 'best' in the middle of a blank A4 sheet, using line guides. Suggest that they are working as designers to make the best use of space on the page. To give the finished poems visual impact, they can use felt-tipped pens to draw birds, bees and butterflies on another sheet of blank paper; then cut these out and stick them around the finished poems. They should glue the bodies onto the border, but leave the wings 'flying' free. (See Figure 3.)

Suggestion(s) for extension
More able children might follow the same structure to make other 'recipe' poems, such as a recipe for autumn or winter, for a storm or for Bonfire Night.

Suggestion(s) for support
Children who find this activity difficult could use photocopiable page 147 as a writing frame. They should fill in each verse with their three ideas set out in a list:

Take some sunshine,
two fluffy clouds
and a soft summer breeze.

Add one swallow,
two lazy lizards
and three bright butterflies.

Simple listing within the recipe headings on this sheet allows less confident children to have almost immediate success in completing a poem. They can go on to illustrate their poem on the photocopied sheet.

Assessment opportunities
Note those children who can use their own ideas to complete each verse, and do not need to 'borrow' from the list on the board. Look for those who have successfully followed the recipe pattern. Note also those children who can extend a line with flair – for example: the sun *burning like a three cheeses pizza on fire...*

Opportunities for IT
You could use the word processor to set up a simple frame for the 'Recipe for Summer' poem so that the children can use it for originating their work on the word processor. This might be particularly helpful for less confident children. The frame might read as follows:

Take a
The
And

Add
Some
And

Mix
Some
And

Bake
For
And you have made SUMMER!

The frame should be saved onto disk, so that children can retrieve it, complete it, rename it for themselves and save it as their own poem.

The children could also print out a class collection of recipe poems. These could be illustrated with pieces of clip art, or presented against the background of a blue summer sky (drawn using an art package) or a summer holiday photograph (or postcard) scanned into the computer.

Display ideas

The children's poems can be backed individually with yellow card and displayed on a blue background, with a painted sun in one corner. Some large painted birds, butterflies and bees can be stuck around the poems, with their bodies glued down and their wings 'free' (as above). This display could be placed above a table with some books about flowers and insects.

Performance ideas

The children can read out or recite their recipe poems in assembly or at a parents' event, wearing chefs' hats made from white paper. They can demonstrate how to use kitchen tools: whisking, stirring and mixing as appropriate, and producing appropriate pictures of the 'baked' summer, winter, storm and so on.

Reference to photocopiable sheet

Photocopiable page 147 is a writing frame which can be used by less confident children to help them complete and illustrate a 'recipe' poem.

ALPHABET POEMS

To use the alphabet as a structure around which to build a poem. To recognize and use alliteration.

†† *Whole-class introduction, individual writing.*

🕐 *40 minutes.*

Previous skills/knowledge needed

The children will need to be familiar with the sequence of the alphabet. They will benefit from having a good grasp of spelling – especially the initial letters of words. They should be able to use a dictionary, have a wide vocabulary, and understand how to go about drafting a written poem.

Key background information

This activity uses the structure of the alphabet to give children confidence in writing a relatively long poem. Children tend to choose easy, 'safe' words for alphabet poems, and it is important that you are ready to prompt them with ideas for more adventurous language. Their completed poems will be mostly humorous in content – though an unexpectedly serious one may creep into the session, and you will need to be sensitive to this.

Before embarking on this activity, it might be helpful to work with the children on some alphabet teasers such as: *What is the letter before T? What are the first two letters after H? What letter is between O and Q?* Make this a quick answer game, with the children themselves firing some of the questions.

Preparation

Find some published examples of alphabet poems, such as 'A-Z of beasts and eats' by John Fairfax (in *Read a poem, Write a poem* edited by Wes Magee, Blackwell 1989), 'A-Z

Writing frame

Recipe for summer

Take _____

_____

and _____

Add _____

_____

and _____

Mix _____

_____

_____

and _____

_____

and _____

Bake _____

_____

and you have made summer!

by _____

of items found on the school roof by the caretaker' by Wes Magee (in *The Witch's Brew*, CUP 1989), 'A listen to this' by John Rice (in *Toughie Toffee* edited by David Orme, Lions 1989), 'A Begins Another' by Julie Holder (in *Crack another Yolk* edited by John Foster, OUP 1996) and 'An Alphabet of Questions' by Charles Edward Carryl (in *Marbles in my Pocket* edited by Moira Andrew, Macmillan (1986).

Find some everyday reference books where the items are given in alphabetical order, such as gardening books, gazetteers, bird-watching books and so on. Make one enlarged (A3) copy per child of photocopiable page 148.

Resources needed

Photocopiable page 148; a board or flip chart; A4 paper, writing materials; dictionaries, thesauruses; poetry anthologies and collections; published alphabet poems (as above); reference books using alphabetical order (as above); an alphabet chart or line (see 'Suggestion(s) for support').

What to do

Start by getting the children to recite the alphabet. Write the letters of the alphabet in order on the flip chart. As an oral exercise, find an animal name for each letter. X is almost impossible, so a bit of cheating is allowed: try *X-cellent elephants*, or resort to the dictionary for *Xenurus* (an armadillo) or *Xenopus* (an African frog).

Give out A3-sized copies of photocopiable page 148. Ask the children to start by writing the letters of the alphabet in order down the first column of the sheet. Next, they should fill in the third column by choosing an animal from the list on the flip chart (or one of their own beginning with the correct letter), so that the sheet looks like this:

A	...	armadillo ...
B	...	bison ...
C	...	cheetah ...

Now ask the children to fill in the spaces on each line with an adjective and a verb (the verb ending with ...*ing*). A draft poem will begin to take shape – for example:

Angry	armadillos	arguing
Bold	bisons	biting
Choosy	cheetahs	chortling ...

Dictionaries are extremely useful for this part of the activity. Encourage the children to be quite adventurous with language. Allow the most able writers to extend their lines, redrafting on a fresh sheet of paper:

> Angry armadillos arguing in the avenue,
> Bold bisons biting their boisterous brothers...

Now suggest 'topping and tailing' the poem: writing first and last lines to put the poem in context. The 'tail' line is optional, but it often serves to complete the piece of writing in a satisfying way. Starting the last line with a linking word such as *And*, *So* or *Then* can help to round off the poem:

> X-cellent Xemas* X-celling with xylophones,
> Yellow yaks yawning into their yoghurt,
> Zig-zag zebras zipping out of the zoo –
> Then all the animals ask to meet YOU!

(***Xema:** a kind of gull)

Once the children are confident with their first A-Z draft, suggest that they work on new A-Z poems. Encourage them to try different sets of things: flowers, birds, first names (using a *Name Your Baby* book or a telephone directory), means of transport, place names and so on.

Another way of looking at alphabet poems is to take a fairly random set of things which all end up in the same place. Wes Magee's 'A-Z of items found on the school roof by the caretaker' could be used as a model for similar list poems: 'A-Z of junk found in the garden shed', 'A-Z of stuff emptied out of my pocket by Mum', and so on.

Encourage the children to think of interesting new topics. For example, an 'A-Z of zany relatives' might start:

> Assorted awful aunties asking to kiss me... again!
> Bothersome baby brothers bashing my brains out.
> Cute country cousins chasing me into the cellar.
> Dreadful dotty Dorothy dreaming all day long...

A class reading and discussion can follow, the children listening with courtesy to their peers' work. If someone has an idea which might help another poet, they should be encouraged to make a suggestion – but the writers are under no obligation to change their work unless they want to! Stress that redrafting is a matter of personal choice.

Suggestion(s) for extension

This structure could lead more able children to attempt a more thoughtful piece, perhaps about their feelings:

A-Z of feelings

Sometimes I'm angry and ache to wave my arms about.
Some days I'm boastful, bang on about being the best!
I can be curious, curling in quiet corners listening.

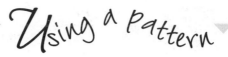
Once I was deceitful and that was a dreadful day.
Sometimes I'm so emotional that I can hardly eat.
When I'm feeling furious I fight friend and foe alike.
Some days I'm so glad I just grin like a gibbon!

Encourage the children to use a dictionary and a thesaurus to help them build a poem of this kind.

Suggestion(s) for support

Children who have difficulty with this activity can be shown an alphabet chart or line for reference. They should be encouraged to work on copies of photocopiable page 148, using a familiar topic (such as bird names) for which it is relatively easy to find a lot of words. They can fill in the words as they think of them, not necessarily working from A through to Z.

These children can gain confidence from working with a more confident partner; the former could think of the nouns and the latter could help with appropriate adjectives and verbs until an A-Z poem gradually emerges.

Assessment opportunities

This activity allows you to judge those who not only know the alphabet, but can use it quickly and effortlessly to find alliterative chains of words. Look for those children who are able to use the alphabetical structure as the basis of a poem. Note those who understand what nouns, verbs and adjectives are; those who can use a wide vocabulary with understanding; and those who display an appreciation of alliteration.

Opportunities for IT

You could set up a starting file with the letters of the alphabet in position for the children to use. This frame could be as simple or detailed as necessary: just the alphabet for some children, the alphabet and suitable animal names for others. The children will need to be able to move the cursor around in order to add words to the poem.

Once the poem has been keyed in, the children could pick out the initial letter for each line and change its font, size or colour. They could extend this to other letters or to the whole line (see Figure 4).

Angry armadillos arguing

Bold bisons biting

Choosy Cheetahs Chortling

Figure 4

Display ideas

The children can display their poems in alphabet books (one letter to a page) or on an alphabet frieze, with appropriate illustrations.

Reference to photocopiable sheet

Photocopiable page 148 provides a ready-made drafting sheet, and will prove particularly useful for those children who need support. It should be copied at A3 size for use.

LETTER POEMS

To empathize with the feelings of a character and communicate these by writing a letter in the form of a poem.

†† *Whole class, pairs, then individual work.*

🕐 *50 minutes.*

Previous skills/knowledge needed

The children should be able to set out a formal letter in the conventional fashion (their letter poems may not necessarily follow this pattern, but the children need to know what they are deviating from). They should be skilled in the initial shaping and redrafting of their work.

Key background information

Writing a poem in the form of a letter gives the children an immediate purpose for writing, as well as a familiar structure within which to work. It can also be useful in bringing a personal element into the teaching of history, helping the children to understand and empathise with people who lived in the past. Taking on the role of one historical character writing to another forces the children to think themselves into another place and another time. Letter poems could also be written as part of a topic on communication.

Preparation

If you are covering a topic on communication, acquire some *The journey of a letter* posters (these are free from the Post Office) and talk the children through the stages from postbox to letterbox. Provide some holiday postcards, and ask the children to bring in some old postcards from home. When you have a collection of these, stick blank removeable labels over the addresses and messages.

Resources needed

Photocopiable page 149: some old postcards (see above); a board or flip chart; writing materials, felt-tipped pens.

What to do

Gather the children together as a class and initiate a discussion on the various means of communication open to us: telephone, letters, faxes, e-mail, video links and so on. Ask them whether they send letters, and why. (To thank relatives for birthday and Christmas presents, perhaps.) Discuss the idea that a letter is permanent and can be kept for many years.

Borrow the school mailbag (if possible) and look at a selection of letters and brochures addressed to the Headteacher. Ask the children: *Do these look different from the kind of mail your parents receive at home? How do people send messages home when they are on holiday? How is a postcard different from a letter?*

Look at some of the old postcards and talk about where they were posted. Note the brighter-than-bright colours of sea and sky, the generally beautiful weather, the smiling people depicted on the cards and so on. Discuss why postcards tend to show images of this kind. Talk about the kind of messages people often write on holiday postcards: *Wish you were here... Weather is terrible/fantastic... Lots to do here... Food is great/awful...* and so on.

Divide the class into pairs and give each pair a coloured holiday postcard. Ask them to look carefully at the picture on the front and then plan a message which describes the scene (without making stock comments such as 'Weather is great' or 'Lots of ice-cream'). Working on paper, the children should make a 'shopping list' of ideas, then draft out a short four- or five-line poem describing the picture. They should head the poem with the first words of a letter (for example, *Dear Mum, Dear Mrs Webb* or *Dear Grandad*), and sign off with their own names. When they are satisfied with the draft, they should write it out in 'best' on the blank labels. For example, a pair might produce the following:

Dear Grandad,
The sand is like golden dust
sprinkled on the shore. The
waves sigh with happiness,
and we ride their backs as if
they were great green dragons.
Love from
    Suzy & Kate

Bring the class back together and ask them to share their work, one child in each pair reading the poem aloud and the other holding up the picture. This part of the activity could have a competitive element, with the class voting on which is the best description.

Point out that these postcard poems have been written by *real* people, imagining themselves in a *real* holiday place. Tell the children that they should now take the idea a stage further by writing a postcard from someone who lived a long time ago. Suggest that Mary, the mother of Jesus, might have written a postcard to the innkeeper and his wife in Bethlehem. If she had, what do they think she might have said? The children can brainstorm ideas for the contents of Mary's postcard: stars, angels, kings, shepherds, the animals, the new baby and so on. Scribe the suggestions on the flip chart.

It will soon become obvious that there are more things to be written than will fit on the back of a postcard – so perhaps Mary wrote a letter instead. Read 'Letter from Egypt' by Moira Andrew (photocopiable page 149) to the children. Explain that here, the poet has tried to think herself inside Mary's head as she writes to thank the innkeeper's wife for letting her and Joseph stay in the stable.

Discuss the poem with the children, asking questions such as: *Could the innkeeper's wife really have been called Miriam? How many shepherds were there? What was Mary wearing? What is the scenery like in Egypt?* Discuss what the poem says about Mary's feelings. Give out copies of the poem and let the children read it silently. Point out that it is written in the form of a letter, beginning *Dear Miriam* and ending *Love to all / at the inn, / Mary.*

Suggest to the children that they choose a character from history and think of a person to whom he or she might write a letter. They should concentrate on the letter-writer's feelings – for example, excited (the first men on the moon, Christopher Columbus), frightened (Joan of Arc, a passenger on the Titanic), lonely (a fighter pilot in the Second World War, an Antarctic explorer). They should think, too, of the clothes the character might be wearing, and how to describe the place he or she is writing from.

The children should work individually, brainstorming their ideas, drafting and then polishing their letter poems.

Suggestion(s) for extension

The most experienced writers could work in pairs, exchanging letters in character. Instead of writing a single letter-poem each, they might produce an extensive correspondence.

Suggestion(s) for support

Children who lack confidence in their writing skills could concentrate on writing their poems on postcards. Using an illustrated history book as reference, they should draw and colour in a postcard-sized picture of, for example, Nelson's *HMS Victory*, then write a short four- or five-line poem on the back. Thus Nelson might have written to his friend Emma, telling her how afraid they all were:

> Dear Emma,
> The sea is rough, waves six feet high.
> The wind is tossing us about like
> empty bottles. With my good eye
> I can see the French ships sailing
> towards us, and I fear for my life.
> I love you dearly,
>> Horatio

This example requires some knowledge of the battle of Trafalgar; but this kind of work helps children to 'step into another person's shoes', and can make history more interesting for them.

Assessment opportunities

Note the children's ability to use the letter form. Note their willingness to think in character, their empathy with the character's feelings, and their ability to express those feelings.

Opportunities for IT

The children could use a word processor to write and present their postcard poems. A desktop publishing package could be set up with two simple frames, one for the poem and the other for the picture. The picture could be added from the children's own pictures created with an art package, scanned from their own line drawings or photographs, or taken from a clip art collection. The children could also experiment with different font styles to make their writing as a historical character more authentic. (See Figure 5.)

If your school has access to e-mail, you could set up a link with another school so that the children can exchange their historical poems. If children in two schools are paired up, they could extend their historical writing by replying to each other's letter poems in the same style.

Figure 5

Display ideas

The finished letter poems can be displayed on a dark background, using coloured tape to indicate correspondence between two people (see 'Suggestion(s) for extension').

Performance ideas

The children can take on the roles of historical characters, using minimal dressing-up props – for example, a paper tricorne hat and eye-patch for Nelson, or a pair of goggles for a Second World War air pilot. They can read out their letter-poems, perhaps adding some role-play.

Reference to photocopiable sheet

The poem on photocopiable page 149 should be used to encourage children to write their own similar 'letter poems' from people in history. They should notice not only the letter format, but also the way in which 'Letter from Egypt' communicates factual details and the feelings of the character. These aspects of the poem should influence the children's own letter poems.

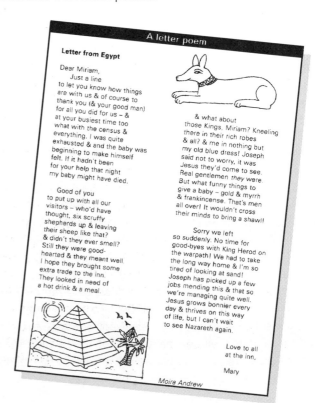

Playing with forms

When you give children the opportunity to work on – and play with – different forms of poetry, you are opening doors to the fun and satisfaction they can gain from using a range of poetic forms. In addition, you are encouraging them to explore traditional patterns of language as a powerful means of expressing their feelings. Each poetic form has its own value and importance. Once you have modelled a new technique, the children can practise it for themselves, using your model as a reference point.

Relatively simple forms such as haiku and acrostics can offer children who need support the safety of a framework in which to write. Low achievers can surprise you when some of the difficulties which they perceive in writing are removed – for example, when the questions *How long should the poem be? How do I know when it is finished? Is this enough?* are answered for them. Despite their brevity, haiku encourage depth of thought and feeling, without requiring much physical effort in handwriting. Acrostics, riddles and shape poems, on the other hand, are really word puzzles, and even the most reluctant writers enjoy the challenge which these forms provide.

Many of the activities in this chapter are more word games than actual poetry writing tasks, but they provide an excellent way of giving children confidence in using language. When the children have mastered some of these techniques, they will develop as writers, able to take the next step towards becoming competent – and perhaps inspired – wordsmiths, familiar with the tools of the trade and knowing how to use them.

POETRY

TURNABOUT POEMS

To develop a wide vocabulary of dramatic expressions, and use them in writing poetry.

†† *Whole class, then individual work.*

⏱ *40 minutes.*

Previous skills/knowledge needed

It will be helpful if the children are familiar with using a thesaurus (but this is not essential). They should have experience of drafting and revising their written work. They should be able to call upon a wide vocabulary.

Key background information

This activity requires the children to use words in an unusual context: words related to a volcano are used to describe the school, a motorway or a supermarket. To be successful, this activity depends on the children's ability to build up a set of related words or synonyms, using a thesaurus if necessary. They should appreciate how words which usually describe one situation can be transferred to another, often with startling effect: language which was descriptive in one context can become idiomatic in another.

Preparation

Collect some illustrated books about (or photographs of) volcanoes. Obtain a picture of a busy street or supermarket (see 'Suggestion(s) for support').

Resources needed

A board or flip chart; writing materials; a thesaurus for each child or small group; books about (or pictures of volcanoes); a picture of a busy street or supermarket (see 'Suggestion(s) for support').

What to do

Introduce the 'turnabout' idea by working with the children as a class. Using a coloured illustration or photograph, encourage the children to think of the awesome power, noise, heat and colour of an erupting volcano. Suggest that they blitz (or brainstorm) all the words they can think of that describe the appearance or sound of a volcano. On the flip chart, scribe the words as they are offered. You might build up a set of words like this:

Volcano

fierce	explode	heat
fiery	erupt	fire
burn	blaze	smoke
ash	furnace	violent

Recourse to the thesaurus will provide more words: *destruction, lava, flare, smoulder, scorch, molten* and so on.

Encourage the children to make their own list of volcano words, using the thesaurus and their own knowledge. You might suggest that verbs are particularly useful – for example, they could look up words related to the verb *to burn*. If necessary, explain how a thesaurus works; make sure the children understand that many possible 'keywords' could be used to find vocabulary related to a given topic.

Give the children a set amount of time to carry out this task (five to ten minutes is usually enough). When they have finished, ask the children to read out the words they have found which are not yet recorded on the flip chart. Add these to the word-blitz.

Explain to the children that they are going to write 'turnabout poems'. They should start with their list of volcano words (with the words from the flip chart added), crossing out the word 'Volcano' at the top and replacing it with either 'School' or 'Motorway'. They can choose either of these topics to write about – but they must use as much of the volcano language as they can. Ask some questions to help them get started:

▲ *Who might erupt in the school?* (The angry teacher, the little children into the playground, the exasperated Head, the bullies, the soccer team onto the pitch...)

▲ *What might turn red or fiery in the school?* (The dinner ladies when a child is rude, your friend when you have made him blush, the PE teacher's face when he tries to keep up with the children...)

▲ *What might burn/scorch down the motorway?* (A police car chasing a stolen van, an ambulance hurrying to an accident, a show-off trying to do the 'ton'...)

Once the children understand how they can use their volcano language in a different context, suggest that they work individually on drafting their poems. You may need to provide opening lines to help some children get started – for example:

POETRY

The little ones erupt
into the playground
when ...

Bully Bert flares with
violence, his fists banging
with ...

Our teacher explodes
with fury, eyes as fiery
as ...

A police car scorches
along the motorway
like ...

Vivid full-length poems will begin to emerge, enhanced by the occasional use of strong and unexpected verbs such as *erupt, melt, scorch, rumble, smoulder, glow, flow, explode, burn* and *blaze*:

High-speed cars erupt
onto the motorway,
melt into the distance,
scorching down the fast lane.

Children rumble and grumble,
smouldering with boredom.
The teacher erupts, smoke
rising from his fiery words,
his eyes glowing with fury.

When they have finished writing, the children could exchange topics with a partner and try again. They could also try writing a poem about a skating rink, a circus or a shopping centre on Christmas Eve – again, using the language of a volcano to describe what they can see in their minds.

Suggestion(s) for extension

More able children could transfer their skills to a different word-blitz and a new topic. For example, they could collect a set of words about rivers: *splash, swirl, current, whirlpool, eddy, surge, meander, waterfall, gush, rush, flood, spill, fish, flow...* Using the 'turnabout' idea, they could use their river language to write about a supermarket, a football match, the rush hour, the end of the school day and so on.

Encourage these children to create vivid descriptions from the words available to them. However, they should not feel trapped by the river words; rather, they should feel liberated to experiment with unusual and exciting language. The following poem is a real example:

Supermarket

Just a trickle at first,
then a flood, then a torrent.
Customers come swirling,
rushing,
gushing
between the banks of food.
Shoppers eager to net
the best bargains are
caught in a whirlpool,
babbling,
bubbling
trolleys sinking underwater.
Now a deluge, wading
to overflowing checkouts,
tills poppling and rippling.
Then a dribble,
just a trickle,
customers draining away,
Closing time!

(Caroline, aged 10)

Suggestion(s) for support

Children who lack confidence in putting pen to paper can work from the volcano blitz on the flip chart. They should look at a picture of a busy street (or supermarket) and pick out words to describe the way that cars, buses, lorries and people are moving along: *flow, roar, gush, zoom...* Help the children to collect sound words (*explode, roar*), colour words (*fiery, smoky*) and so on. Encourage responses such as:

Cars zoom along the street,
lights blazing,
exhaust smoking,
engine roaring.
Crowds of people flow past
like hot lava,
tongues babbling,
tempers flaring.

Assessment opportunities

Note those children who show interest in language, and whose vocabulary is extensive. Look for those who find the task of using words in a new context too difficult. Note those children who can use a thesaurus with ease and confidence.

Opportunities for IT

Some children could use a word processor to create and draft their poems. The emphasis should be on crafting their work: looking for better descriptive words or improving the form of the poem. The finished poems could be presented as a class book, possibly with pictures added to the computer file. The pictures could show a volcano, or aspects

of the school that the poem is describing. Photographs of the school could be taken with a digital camera; or printed photographs could be scanned.

Display ideas
Ask the children to draw a volcano outline and copy out their poems in 'best' inside it. They can then colour in the volcano with red, orange and yellow felt-tipped pens, drawing flames and sparks around the top, but taking care to leave the writing visible.

Performance ideas
The dramatic nature of 'turnabout' poems means that they lend themselves well to being read aloud, with background music played on percussion instruments.

HAIKU

To appreciate the haiku form and to write poems in that form, selecting the words carefully.

†† *Whole class, groups of three, then individual work.*
🕐 *40 minutes.*

Previous skills/knowledge needed
The children should be familiar with the concept of a syllable. They should be used to drafting and editing their own written work, and they should have had some practice in recognizing and using images.

Key background information
Haiku are short formal poems of a kind first developed in Japan. They are written to a very strict pattern, based on a syllable count. The English version of a haiku has a pattern of 5–7–5 syllables (in three lines). It works best if there is one main image – and every word needs to count. A haiku should surprise the reader and make him or her look with new eyes at an everyday scene.

Despite its brevity, the haiku form is not an easy option. However, many children have such a fresh outlook that they can use the seventeen syllables of a haiku to paint unusually vivid word-pictures.

Preparation
To give the children practice in counting syllables, suggest that they form groups according to the number of syllables in their first names (thus David would be in the same group as Sarah, Mark in the same group as Kate, and so on). Make a simple graph based on the number of children in each group. Find some poetry anthologies which include examples of haiku in English – for example: *Crack Another Yolk* edited by John Foster (OUP, 1966); *This Poem Doesn't Rhyme* edited by Gerard Benson (Viking, 1990).

Resources needed
Anthologies of poetry including haiku; a board or flip chart; writing materials; strips of paper (A4 cut into three lengthways).

What to do
Start with the children grouped according to the number of syllables in their first names (see above). Ask each group to make up a rhythmic chant, clapping to each syllable in their names. Next, ask them to think of a different number and think of flower names, place names and so on with that number of syllables; again, suggest that they work on a rhythmic chant, clapping to the syllable-count.

Building on the syllable work suggested above, introduce the concept of a *haiku* as a short, concentrated word-picture in three lines with five syllables in the first, seven in the second and five in the third. The children will usually be intrigued and see the composition of a haiku as an interesting puzzle to be solved. Tell them that a haiku often begins with a suggestion of the time of day, season or place. Read out and discuss a few examples from anthologies.

Ask for possible first lines and collect them on the flip chart – for example:

In the summer air	In the morning sun
In a forest glade	On the mountain top
Down our busy street	When winter snow falls

Divide the children into new groups of three and pass out a strip of paper to each child. Ask them either to write a five-syllable line implying *where* or *when* something is (for example, *Down in the cellar*) or to choose a line from the flip chart. When they have finished, ask them to pass on the paper to the next person in the group. When they have read the first line, they should work on a second which goes on to tell, in seven syllables, *who* or *what* is involved – for example:

In the summer air
flowers open petals wide

When winter snow falls
cold winds whistle through the trees

Now for the really difficult bit! The children should pass on the paper again and complete the haiku with a word-picture in five syllables. It sometimes helps to suggest that the last line might begin with the word *like*. This makes it fairly easy to invent an image – for example:

In the summer air
flowers open petals wide
like butterflies' wings
or like painted pictures
or like bright coloured inks.

When winter snow falls
cold winds whistle through the trees
like ghosts out to play
or like a storm at sea
or like howling banshees.

The groups should read their haiku aloud to the class. Choose some that go together and rewrite them as a set on the flip chart. A sequence of five or more related haiku is known as a *renga*.

Use the flip chart to present a range of possible haiku titles. Make specific suggestions – for example: *Blackbird, Owl, Kestrel, Panther, Giraffe, Elephant, Shower, Storm, Rainbow, Winter, Autumn, Summer* and so on. Indicate that these titles relate to general themes such as seasons, weather and animals.

Now ask the children to work individually, choosing a title from the flip chart or thinking of something similar within the themes you have suggested. Remind them of the syllable count, 5–7–5, and that their haiku should paint a vivid picture in words.

Suggestion(s) for extension

Children who are confident writers could work individually to make up a renga with five or more related haiku.

Alternatively, they could try writing a familiar story in the form of a set of haiku – for example:

In a dark kitchen
Cinderella worked all day
till her hands were sore.

Two ugly sisters
made Cinders work harder still
to keep the house clean.

Then a letter came
'Please attend the Palace Ball'
Cinders cried and cried.

'I can't go like this!'
she said. But the sisters laughed,
'Who invited you?'
　　　　　　　...and so on.

This narrative task could be shared among a group who work well together. Before they begin, they should draw up a basic storyboard and decide which part of the story each poet should tackle. The completed haiku story could be presented as an illustrated zigzag book.

These children can also use the poetry anthologies to find examples of haiku. They can copy these into class day books and anthologies.

Suggestion(s) for support

An adult helper who is ready to support and encourage children will do wonders for those who lack confidence in their own abilities. Let the children use their fingers to count out the syllables. Write out a few possible five-syllable opening lines from which they can choose. Lines which have worked well in this context include:

On a sandy beach　　　　Down by the river
In the sparkling waves　　One snowy morning

Encourage the children to work as a group, exploring the possibilities of the next two lines. For example, working from the first idea above, they might try:

On a sandy beach
children laugh and run about
(*or* mothers watch the children play
or we lie down on our towels)
under the hot sun.
(*or* until it gets late.
or in the bright sunshine.)

Within this simple structure, each child in the group can contribute towards a shared word-picture.

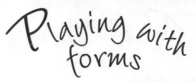
Assessment opportunities

Note those children who find it easy to combine all the factors necessary to write a successful haiku: brevity, clarity, good use of imagery and an ability to adjust the wording until the correct syllable-count has been achieved – no mean feat! Look out for those who stick to one way of writing a line, and thus have difficulty in changing phrases to fit the pattern.

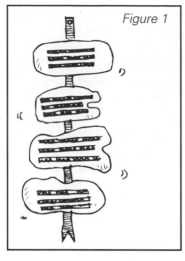

Figure 1

IT opportunities

The word processor lends itself well to the writing of haiku, as there are few words in a verse and the children can concentrate on the style and the form rather than the physical task of typing. The children could separate the syllables, so that the computer reads each one as a single word. This will make it easier to keep track of the number of syllables used, since the poem should have a word count of 17:

> In the summ er air
> Flow ers op en pet als wide
> Like butt er flies' wings.

The syllables within each word could be joined up again once the poem is completed.

Children who are writing individual haiku on similar themes could merge them together on screen to form a renga. To do this, they will need to save their own haiku to a disk, and then insert them into the final version – either by using the inset file command or by dragging and dropping the file into the word processor. Alternatively, the children could *cut and paste* their haiku from their own files into the growing renga.

Display ideas

Haiku lend themselves well to a layered mobile display. Ask each child to write his or her own poem out in 'best' on thin card or art paper. This can be shaped like a mountain, lake, garden or shore scene, or cut out into the shape of a bird or animal, as appropriate. The shape should always be irregular. The background to the poem should be filled in using coloured pencils – very faintly, so that the writing is not obscured. The haiku should be strung downwards on a ribbon (see Figure 1). A layered mobile is ideal in a crowded classroom where the display area is limited.

RIDDLES

To explore 'riddle' poems and identify their typical features. To write their own riddle poems for a peer audience.

†† *Whole class, groups or pairs, then individual work.*

🕘 *40 minutes.*

Previous skills/knowledge needed

The children will benefit from having worked on image poems (see 'Images of the moon', page 48). They should have practice in solving word-puzzles such as simple crosswords. They should be familiar with the skills of drafting and editing their own writing. They should also be willing to read their work aloud, and feel confident about sharing it with others in the class.

Key background information

Riddles are basically word-puzzles. Children enjoy the detective element involved in solving them, and even the most reluctant writers are keen to take part in creating word-puzzles and guessing the answer. Riddles were part of everyday life in past times, long before writing was invented: they were passed on by word of mouth. They take many forms, and are found in cultures all over the world. At one time, a riddle and its solution were thought to have magical properties; in traditional fairy stories, it often falls to the hero to solve a difficult riddle before he is allowed to marry the king's daughter.

Preparation

Obtain some anthologies or collections of poetry which include riddles, such as *Crack Another Yolk* by John Foster (OUP, 1966). Make one copy per child of photocopiable page 150.

Resources needed

Anthologies or collections of poetry which include riddles; a board or flip chart; writing materials; photocopiable page 150.

What to do

Gather the children together as a class. Tell them that they are going to play the role of detective: you have some word-puzzles for them to solve. Read aloud some of the traditional riddles from photocopiable page 150, and see whether the children can guess the answers.

Tell them that the following puzzle is from ancient Greece, and is one of the oldest riddles known:

> What goes on four legs in the morning,
> two legs in the afternoon
> and three legs in the evening?

This is quite a difficult riddle to solve, but it will help the children get into the 'detective' way of thinking. Explain to them that a riddle hides a picture of itself inside other pictures or images, like a distorting mirror at a fairground. Help them to look for clues: *What does 'in the morning' mean? What about 'in the afternoon' and 'in the evening'? If it means 'in the morning (afternoon, evening) of life', does this help?*

Allow time for them to discuss the problem until either they have to ask for another clue or someone realizes the answer! Take time to explain the solution in some detail: people crawling on all fours as babies, walking on two legs as adults, needing a stick when they are old.

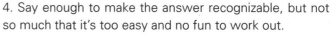

Once they have begun to see how riddles work, the children will be anxious to have another go. Give out copies of photocopiable page 150 and look at the first of these riddles together: *A wee wee man...* If the children need a clue, tell them to think of different kinds of fruit. (The answer is a cherry.) Work through the next three riddles together, helping with additional clues if necessary, but encouraging careful thought.

Ask the class whether anyone knows a riddle which might catch the others out. They may remember a traditional one from home; or they could look one up in an anthology. Allow about five minutes for these riddles to be posed and solved.

Now use the flip chart to show the children the first steps in making up a riddle. Ask them for images to describe the stars: *drawing pins, bubbles, confetti, snowflakes, diamonds* and so on. Use some of their ideas to make up a simple image poem using similes – for example:

Stars are like drawing pins
stuck in the blackboard.
They are like bubbles
floating into space.
Stars are like snowflakes
spinning in the sky.
They are like diamonds
sparkling on a velvet top.

On the flip chart, show how this image poem can be changed into a riddle. Remind the children that they must not give away the solution, but should just give a set of clues. In this case, they should cross out *Stars* and *They* and substitute *We*, so the poem begins: *We are like drawing pins...* The riddle could end with the question *What are we?* This is an example of an 'outside-in' image poem.

Next, the children can try to write some riddles for themselves, working in pairs or groups. They should discuss some possible topics that would be fun to write about. Suggest that they think about things that are visible in the classroom or outside the window, such as an animal, the weather or a machine.

Once the children have made their choice of subject, suggest some working rules that will make the writing easier. Note these on the flip chart:

1. Don't give the game away by giving the poem a title.
2. Start by using either 'I' or 'We' – that is, writing in the first person, as though the answer to the riddle were describing itself.
3. Describe the mystery thing accurately in six or eight short lines, perhaps writing an 'outside-in' image poem to start off with.
4. Say enough to make the answer recognizable, but not so much that it's too easy and no fun to work out.

Once the groups have made up at least one riddle, let them try it out on other groups. Encourage the children to think of themselves as detectives, solving a set of clues. Help those who have made their poems too easy or too difficult, explaining that they need to describe with accuracy, but in a way that makes the thing being described sound strange. For example, is *I weave patterns in the air* about a plane, a kite, the wind? How do these new lines help?

We scribble on the dark
with felt-tipped pens,
weave patterns in the air.
We bloom and fade and fall,
our brief lives
scattered over the earth
in a silver fall of sparks.
What are we?

Now that they have had some practice, ask the children to work individually and write riddles on their own. Remind them to think of the ways that things move and feel, their colours and sounds, and to make up images which bring these details to life.

Help anyone who is stuck by suggesting some interesting subjects for a riddle: *a dragon, an earth mover, a tin opener, a tea bag, a frisbee, a cricket bat, a CD, a dictionary, the moon, stars, the sun, fog, holly, icicles...*

When the children have finished, let them exchange riddles with their friends. Have a competition to find the best riddle – which is not the most difficult, but the most interesting to think about.

Suggestion(s) for extension

Children who are experienced writers might like to try writing more sophisticated riddles. They could write longer riddles with three or four verses describing the same thing through related images – for example:

> We dance in our coloured shoes,
> pirouetting away from arms
> that once held us safe.
>
> Our green veins run cold,
> we are brittle boats sailing
> on the cold bright air.
>
> We settle in drifts, crackling
> underfoot, whispering together
> in dry throaty voices.

The thread of a single theme runs through the images in these three verses: autumn leaves. The images describe three different stages: the leaves breaking away, falling, settling on the ground.

Some traditional riddles are made by hiding letters of the alphabet within the lines of a poem. Writing riddles in this way is quite a difficult task, but more confident children may enjoy the challenge. An example is shown below:

Power

> My first is in flame,
> but not in spark,
> my second in light,
> not in the dark.
> My third is in flicker,
> but not in night,
> my last in candle,
> but not in bright.
> My whole is orange
> and yellow and red,
> without me, the world
> would long be dead.
> What am I?

Moira Andrew

Show the children how to work out the answer to this riddle. The first letter is found in *flame*, but not in *spark*. Thus it can't be A, which is common to both. It could be F, L, M or E. After the four clues to individual letters, there are two clues to the whole word. Perhaps the language of the first eight lines provides more clues... The children should be able to work out that the hidden word is *fire*.

The children might look in the anthologies for further examples of this kind of riddle – such as 'My first is in ...' by John Kitching, from *My First Has Gone Bonkers* edited by Brian Moses (Blackie, 1993).

Suggestion(s) for support

Children who are having problems with writing should concentrate on simple image riddles. The sun, the moon, clouds and stars work well as themes – for example:

> I am like a white ship
> sailing across the sky.
> I am like a plump cushion
> on a blue chair.
> What am I?   *(Answer: a cloud.)*

Assessment opportunities

Note the children's ability to work with images, and their enthusiasm for using language in a creative way. Look for those who show skill in solving word-puzzles.

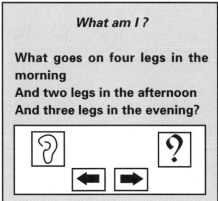

Figure 2

Opportunities for IT

The children could use a multi-media authoring package to make an interactive display of their completed riddles. Each child or pair should be given two pages of the presentation to use. On the first page, they should write their riddle. (This may already have been written on a word processor, in which case it can be inserted without retyping it.) The children can format their text to make it look exciting, and change the font styles and sizes to fill the page; however, they should be careful about adding pictures that might give away the answer. The second page should contain the answer to the riddle, in the form of a word or a suitable picture. Figure 2 shows an example.

The children then need to link the answer page to the riddle – perhaps by placing a large question mark on the page which functions as an icon: when you click on it, you are shown the answer page. The children could extend the activity by adding a spoken version of their riddle. This can be recorded using a microphone attached to the computer; the riddle page could have an ear or other symbol which the user should click on in order to hear the riddle.

The oldest or most able pupils might like to set up the presentation so that the riddle is displayed a section at a

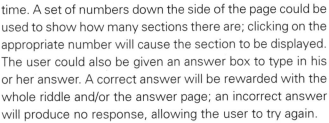

Figure 3

time. A set of numbers down the side of the page could be used to show how many sections there are; clicking on the appropriate number will cause the section to be displayed. The user could also be given an answer box to type in his or her answer. A correct answer will be rewarded with the whole riddle and/or the answer page; an incorrect answer will produce no response, allowing the user to try again.

Where children are new to this type of IT application, the structure of the presentation should be set up by the teacher to begin with. A title page can be created, with the name of each child or group shown. By clicking on a particular name, the user is taken to that riddle. The pages will also need to have 'forward' and 'back' arrows, to take the user on to the next riddle or back to the start.

Display ideas
The children can use A4 sheets of thin card to display individual riddles. They should fold the card into four (as shown in Figure 3), then copy out the riddle on the left-hand inside page. The answer can be written beneath a flap on the right-hand page. They should write a title on the front – not giving away the answer, but perhaps giving a clue (for example, *Riddle of the night* or *Riddle of winter*).

Reference to photocopiable sheet
The four traditional riddles given on photocopiable page 150 should be read out to the class and discussed; then the sheet should be given to the children and the riddles worked through with teacher guidance. The solutions are as follows: a cherry; snow and sun; your hair; clouds.

ACROSTICS

To recognize the acrostic form in poetry and understand its uses. To write poems in this style and polish them through redrafting.

†† *Groups, whole class, then group work.*

🕐 *40 minutes.*

Previous skills/knowledge needed
This activity relies on children being able to picture and itemize the characteristics of the topic (a month, season, weather, animal and so on) they choose to write about. They should also be able to spell correctly, and to manipulate words and phrases to fit into the required form.

Key background information
Acrostics are often regarded as an easy option by teachers, but they require a certain amount of skill with using words and some knowledge of the chosen topic. The title is spelt out by the initial letters of the lines, reading downward; the poem's theme should also be reflected in the content. Children often enjoy solving or creating acrostic puzzles; but an effective acrostic poem is more difficult to write than might appear at first sight. Seasons, weathers, months, games, occupations, countries, personalities and so on – that is, things with distinctive names and features – make good subjects for acrostics.

Playing with forms

Preparation

Make one copy per child of photocopiable page 151, and some copies of photocopiable page 152 (see 'Suggestion(s) for support'). Obtain some books with examples of acrostic poems – for example: *Crack Another Yolk* edited by John Foster (OUP, 1996); *Read a Poem, Write a Poem* edited by Wes Magee (Blackwell 1989). Obtain a calendar with seasonal illustrations.

Resources needed

A calendar (see above); photocopiable pages 151 and 152; books with acrostic poems; a board or flip chart; writing materials.

What to do

Introduce the activity by showing the children the illustrated calendar and using it to stimulate discussion of the seasons. Divide the class into groups and ask each group to write lists of the weather, games, clothes and so on that they associate with each month of the year. (Each group should make as many lists as possible.) Ask the children to put their lists aside; they will need to refer to them later on.

Bring the class back together. Read out one of Moira Andrew's acrostic poems from photocopiable page 151. Discuss its content and establish that the poem describes the month named in the title. Give out copies of the page, and elicit the observation that the initial letters of the lines spell out the name of the month. Tell the children that this form of poem is called an *acrostic*.

Ask the children to refer to their word lists and suggest things that they associate with the month of October, such as *cold winds, fallen leaves, migrating birds* and *half-term holidays*. List some of their ideas on the flip chart. Now scribe the word OCTOBER downwards and, taking suggestions from the children, try to fill in lines using some of their ideas. You need to keep two ideas going simultaneously: using the initial letters to start the lines and describing the characteristics of the month in the poem.

Remind the class that the first version written down won't be a finished poem. It will almost certainly need to be altered, with words changed or moved around. Let the children see you crossing out, using arrows and so on, so that the necessary drafting process becomes visible. The following example shows the progress to an improved (and very different) draft, perhaps by way of intermediate drafts:

Owls hooting in the night → Oak trees shedding their leaves.
Colours changing → Cold winds blowing
Towering trees → Thick coats
On holiday → Orange lanterns for Hallowe'en
Birds migrating to warmer shores
Elderberries big and black → Elm trees standing tall
Red berries in the woods → Robin redbreasts

Point out that the acrostic form can be made more obvious by adopting an *O is for owls...* pattern. With the children's help, construct a poem with this format – for example:

O is for owls swooping
C is for cold winds blowing
T is for tall trees creaking
O is for orange lanterns glowing
B is for blackbirds winging
E is for elderberries ripening
R is for raindrops pattering

Now divide the children into groups and suggest that each group works on a different month, so that you can make a class calendar of acrostics. They can use some of the lines on the flip chart to help them. If they wish, they can use the *O is for...* format; alternatively, they can go straight into the poem – for example:

Frost sparkles on
Every bare black
Branch, every fence post.
Robins fluff their feathers
Under the lacy trees,
All brave in coats
Red as holly berries, but
Yearning for spring.

Children who finish this activity early should try writing acrostics for the days of the week or the seasons of the year. The following example is by Michael Richards, from *Writing Poems* by Michael Harrison and Christopher Stuart-Clark (OUP, 1985).

Monday

Moon's Day: the first day
Ought to shine in the week like
New minted silver.
Dull copper thoughts just
Add another penny to
Yesterday's small change.

Further examples that could be discussed include 'Simple seasons' by Eric Finney and 'Holidays' by John Foster (both in *Read a Poem, Write a Poem* edited by Wes Magee).

Suggestion(s) for extension

Children who are more accomplished writers could try acrostics based on 'things people say', such as GOODBYE, I LOVE YOU or HAPPY BIRTHDAY. The content of such an acrostic poem should reflect the moods and circumstances of the person writing and/or receiving it. The acrostic message could be 'hidden' by having a different title, or no title. Here is I LOVE YOU as an acrostic:

I myself and me
L ike you a lot, think
O f you often,
V ery often,
E very day, in fact,
Y esterday, today and
O f course, tomorrow –
U ntil someone nicer comes along!

Suggestion(s) for support

Suggest to children who need help and support that they write 'single-word acrostics': acrostic poems with one word on each line. For example:

Rainbow
R ain's
A rch
I s a
N arrow
B ridge
O ver
W ater

(The odd bit of cheating is allowed, as in *Is a*.)

These children might also benefit from using photocopiable page 152 as a writing frame to help them create seasonal acrostic poems.

Assessment opportunities

Note those children who can tease out the most important elements of a subject and assemble them into the required poetic form. Note those who have the tenacity to work on their poem, using redrafting techniques, until it fits the pattern and reads smoothly.

Opportunities for IT

The children could use a word processor to write their own acrostic poems, highlighting the initial letter of each line by changing its size or colour. They could experiment with using a different font for the initial letter, or even using clip art fonts to make a simple illuminated letter at the start of each line (see Figure 4).

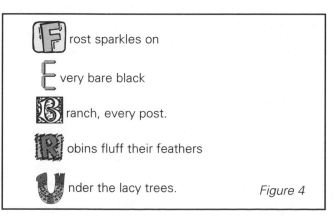

F rost sparkles on
E very bare black
B ranch, every post.
R obins fluff their feathers
U nder the lacy trees.

Figure 4

R ain's
A rch
I s a
N arrow
B ridge
O ver
W ater

Figure 5

Display ideas

Look for pictures of medieval illuminated manuscripts in reference books, and suggest that the children use felt-tipped pens to highlight the initial letters of their acrostic poems in an 'illuminated script' style. (See Figure 5.)

Reference to photocopiable sheets

The three acrostic poems given on photocopiable page 151 can be discussed as examples of the form.

Photocopiable page 152 can be used for support as a writing frame: children who find setting up an acrostic poem difficult can fill in the blanks on this sheet (see 'Suggestion(s) for support').

SEQUENCES

To use a sequential framework to write a poem. To identify and use alliteration.

†† *Four groups, whole class, then individual work.*

🕐 *50 minutes.*

Previous skills/knowledge needed

For this activity, the children need to be aware of the basic sequences that structure our lives: the hours of the day, the days of the week, the seasons and so on. They should also be able to consider and think through more complicated sequences, such as the development from birth to old age. They should be familiar with drafting and editing skills.

Key background information

The simple ideas about sequencing explored in this activity allow writers of all abilities to produce a satisfactory poem.

Working initially with four verses based on the seasons, the more sophisticated writer can go on to work on a more complex poem – with the reassurance that the structure is already mapped out. The appeal of this structure, even to experienced poets, is reflected in the number of excellent sequence poems which exist in print.

Preparation

Make one copy per child of photocopiable page 153. Find some books which include a range of sequence poems – for example, Wes Magee's 'A week of winter weather' (in

The Witch's Brew and Other Poems, OUP 1989), Anthony Thwaite's 'A haiku yearbook' (in *Poetry Street 1* edited by David Orme and James Sale, Longman 1990) and John Foster's 'Month by month' (in *Four o'clock Friday*, OUP 1991).

Resources needed

Photocopiable page 153; a current calendar; a board or flip chart; writing materials; a thesaurus for each child or small group; some anthologies or collections of poetry (see above).

What to do

Give each child a copy of 'Sea seasons' (photocopiable page 153). Divide the class into four groups, and ask each group to look closely at a different verse of the poem. Ask each group in turn to read the first line of their verse. The four opening lines all start with *The sea...* ; the verses go on to describe how the sea moves in each season of the year.

Now ask the children to look more closely at the way in which 'Sea seasons' is written, with one verse to each season. What can they say about the use of 'b' sounds in the first verse, 's' sounds in the second verse, and so on? Discuss the use of alliteration in the poem, and its effect on the sound of each verse.

Tell the children that 'Sea seasons' is an example of a *sequence poem*. Ask them to cut it up into four separate verses and explore different possible sequences. Ask: *Why do some of these sequences work better than others? Is the best sequence the original one? Why?*

Work with the whole class on the next part of the activity. Using the calendar, gather other possible sequences – hours of the day, days of the week, months of the year, the numbers 1 to 10 and so on – on the flip chart. Using these sequences, guide the children towards working on a seasons poem which starts with *In the playground, In the garden, On the shore, In the park* or something similar. For example:

> In the garden
> daffodils dance/tulips tiptoe/crocuses curtsey
> through the cool days
> of spring.

> In the garden
> sunflowers samba/roses romp/lilies loiter
> through the hot days
> of summer.

Working in groups, in pairs or as individuals, the children can make up a seasons sequence using one or all of these ideas. Suggest using a thesaurus, and encourage an ambitious use of alliterative verbs.

The children can share their finished poems by reading

their work aloud to the others in the class. A group or pair could practise reading a verse each to make up an evenly-paced duet or ensemble performance.

Some children might like to find published examples of sequence poems (see 'Preparation') and use some of these poems as a stimulus to write their own similar poems. They could read out or recite some of the published poems in groups or pairs, as above.

Suggestion(s) for extension

Children who have finished ahead of their classmates could try planning and writing more sophisticated sequence poems – for example, describing a food, colour and mood for each day of the week; or describing a game, festival and outfit for each month of the year. They may prefer to make their poems rhyme – for example:

Food for the week
Sausages for Monday,
brown and sizzling hot.
Curry's the dish for Tuesday,
all spicy from the pot... and so on.

The most confident writers could make up their own sequence – for example: *When the sun shines... / When the wind blows... / When the mist shivers...*

The children could also write a sequence poem about growing up or growing old, perhaps using the photographs in a family album for ideas. Again, suggest that they establish a pattern in the writing – for example:

When Granny was a baby,
she wore a white shawl,
smiled in her father's arms.

When Granny was a toddler,
she wore a lacy dress,
sat on her mother's knee.

When Granny was a little girl,
she wore ...
stood ...

The children could also use scientific and other topic books to generate ideas for sequence poems: *From spawn to frog, From egg to butterfly, From rain to tap, The countdown to spring*, and so on.

Suggestion(s) for support

Children who need help with independent writing could benefit from using a simple 'seasons' format, with four verses which follow the same pattern. For example, a sequence poem following an apple tree through the seasons might look like this:

The apple tree

The blossom is pink,
pink and pretty
in spring.

The leaves are green,
green and glossy
in summer.

The apples are red,
red and ripe
in autumn.

The branches are black,
black and bare
in winter.

These children should have the opportunity to read out their finished work along with everyone else.

Assessment opportunities

Note those children who can find and follow through a sequence, working independently. Note those who find it easy to build up an effective writing format, and those who show the ability to use alliteration.

Opportunities for IT

You could set up a simple 'sequence poem' writing frame on the word processor to assist children who find it difficult to get started – for example:

When granny was a baby
She wore ...
smiled ...

When granny was a toddler
She wore ...
sat ...   (and so on)

Older or more able pupils might like to make up their own structure and save it to a disk for others to use.

Completed poems could be presented using a word processor or desktop publishing package, with suitable illustrations added from scanned line drawings, photographs or clip art to give a pictorial view of the sequence.

Display ideas

The four-verse seasons poems will fit well into a zigzag format, with the title on the front folded-back page and a verse copied out and illustrated on each of the following pages. (See Figure 6.) Alternatively, the poem could be

Figure 6

SHAPE POEMS

To compare different styles of shape poems (concrete poems and calligrams). To experiment with writing shape poems. To develop skills in written presentation of work.

†† *Whole class, then individual work.*

🕐 *55 minutes.*

Previous skills/knowledge needed

The children should have looked at the use of images in poetry. They should be able to draft and reappraise their work, and be willing to persevere with manipulating words and phrases until they fit into the shape they envisage. Prior work on making shapes with the body in PE lessons would be useful – for example, using arms to model the differences in shape between an oak tree and a fir tree.

Key background information

Shape poems fall into two main categories. In a **calligram**, the way in which the letters are written or printed represents an aspect of the poem's theme – for example, a poem about fear could be written in shaky handwriting or printed in 'distressed text'. In a **concrete poem**, the layout of the words on the page represents an aspect of the poem's theme – for example, in a poem about a crowded place, the words could be printed without spaces.

Children usually respond enthusiastically to the challenge of creating shape poems. This activity requires them to use language in highly imaginative ways. It is a two-stage process: after working on the words of a poem, the children experiment with different ways of displaying it on the page to reflect the shape and/or movement of the poem's subject. This task also places emphasis on the children's ability to present their written work in an attractive way.

Preparation

Make copies (one of each per child) of photocopiable pages 154 and 155. Make some copies of photocopiable page 156 and cut out the individual 'starters' as strips – enough to provide one strip per child. Collect some illustrations and photographs of various things – such as birds, fireworks, snakes, trees, bridges, trains and so on – which might make interesting subjects for shape poems. Find some books – such as *Madtail, Miniwhale* edited by Wes Magee (Viking Kestrel, 1989) – with examples of shape poems.

displayed on an A4 sheet divided into four sections, with a verse and illustration in each section. Longer sequence poems, such as those based on days of the week or months of the year, can be displayed on long hanging zigzags (rather like the old-fashioned fold-up postcards).

Reference to photocopiable sheet

Photocopiable page 153 shows a 'sequence' poem which uses images to follow changes in time. It can be used as a stimulus for children's own descriptive sequence poems.

Resources needed

Illustrations and photographs (see above); a board or flip chart; writing materials, including black italic writing pens and fine-pointed felt-tipped pens; photocopiable pages 154, 155 and 156; poetry anthologies and collections with examples of shape poems.

What to do

Start with the whole class. Ask the children to suggest six things they know about a bat (or a snake, or a caterpillar) and scribe their suggestions on the flip chart – for example: *A bat comes out at night, it hangs upside down, it swoops as it flies, it has wide wings like an umbrella, it eats insects on the wing, it avoids objects in the dark by using a kind of radar.* Show how you can assemble a poem from these disparate ideas:

Bats

Creatures of the night
swooping and gliding
on umbrella wings.
Radar-guided, snatching
an insect snack before
roosting upside down
to wait for moon-rise.

Show the children some pictures of bats flying, and draw a flying bat outline on the flip chart. Arrange the words and phrases along the outline, as shown in Figure 7. Alternatively, demonstrate how to make a snake or caterpillar poem in the same way.

Use the flip chart to work on another topic (for example, fireworks), using the same method. Start by brainstorming the children's movement and image phrases:

Fireworks

fizzing like sherbet
jumping like beans
whizzing like frisbees
whirling like ribbons
swooping like owls
screaming like banshees
zipping like racing cars
dying in a shower of sparks

Now use the flip chart to arrange these lines in a way that suggests a firework display. Figure 8 shows an example.

Give out the poem 'Snake' by Moira Andrew (photocopiable page 154). Discuss the ways in which the poet has arranged the words into a shape or picture poem. Ask: *Do the words themselves add to the effect of the poem?* Elicit responses such as: *The repetition of the letter S suggests a snake hissing.*

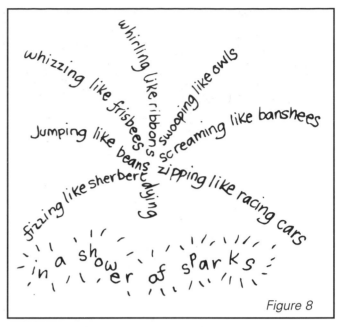

Figure 8

The short words in the first verse suggest quick, sudden movement.

Now give out 'Poem' by Moira Andrew (photocopiable page 155). Discuss the ways in which this poem uses the arrangement of words to suggest not only shape, but also movement: stepping up and down, meandering and falling. Part of it even suggests the frustration of not being able to move! Discuss how the poet might have described flying: can the children suggest a suitable line with the words arranged to suggest wings or an aeroplane? Could they write the actual *letters* in ways that suggest movement? (For example, writing in exaggeratedly slanted italics, stretched-out letters, bouncy 3D letters.)

These listening and looking tasks set the scene for work on composing shape poems which start with written images. Give out one 'starter' strip per child (cut from photocopiable page 156) When the children have had time to look at these, give out some unlined A4 paper. Explain that each child should use his or her starter strips to provide the first line of an image poem – for example:

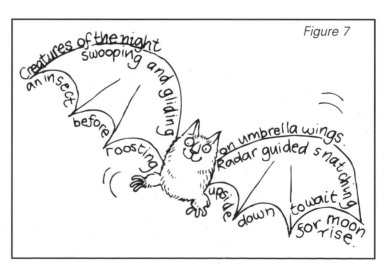

Figure 7

Stars glittering like diamonds,
winking like bright eyes
flickering like candle flames
twinkling like dancers' feet
shining like gold coins
beaming like headlights
from a dark night sky.

Now ask the children to use the A4 paper to rough out an appropriate shape for their own image poem. Explain that they should arrange their words and phrases to make the shape; thus the 'star' image poem above could be arranged to make a pattern of stars, as in Figure 9.

When the children have completed this part of the activity, let them develop their poems by incorporating other 'shape' techniques such as distorted letters, rearranged letters and words repeated on the page (to give a 3D effect). Finally, the children should write out their picture poems in 'best' using italic writing pens or fine felt-tipped pens. Remind them to concentrate on their skills of presentation.

Some children might like to find examples of published concrete poems or calligrams (see 'Preparation' above), and try to use similar techniques in their own poems.

Suggestion(s) for extension

More able children could work on shape poems suggested by the weather: rain, clouds, a rainbow, lightning and so on. The words in different lines could be arranged to suggest different kinds of weather.

Suggestion(s) for support

Children who are struggling with this activity may enjoy working on single-letter poems! They could look at the alphabet and see which letters sound like a whole word: B (bee), C (sea), I (eye), P (pea), Q (queue), U (you) and T (tea). Next, they should think of a way of using these letters to make a simple word puzzle – for example, *B hive, T time* or *U R my best friend*. Suggest that they draw, for example, a hive or a pot of honey with a swarm of **B**s buzzing around it, or a bus stop with lots of **Q**s standing patiently in line.

Figure 9

Assessment opportunities

Note those children who can use written images in a lively way; those who can see the possibilities of shaping words and phrases to show appropriate movement and pattern; and those whose presentational skills are of a high order.

Opportunities for IT

Some children might like to present their shape poems using a word processor to set out the shape. This is one occasion when they will need to use the space bar, not the formatting commands, to shape their poem. Most word processors restrict the user to laying text out in lines, and the children will need to experiment to make their poem into the shape they want. Some frame-based word processors and desktop publishing programs allow the user to treat each line of text as a separate 'object', which can be moved to wherever the child wants it on the page; some even allow the text to be rotated.

An alternative way to create shape poems on screen is to use a drawing package which allows text to be shaped in different ways. Each line of the poem needs to be keyed in as a separate object. Each text object can then be stretched, squashed, rotated, twisted or made to fit a particular shape of pathway. The children will enjoy experimenting with this type of software. They should,

however, be shown how to use the *undo* button, since the effects of the changes can be unexpected and they may need to get back to where they were!

In both of these activities, the children can alter the background of their shape poem, setting the poem against an appropriate picture or pattern.

Display ideas
The children's shape poems or word pictures can be written in black ink on white paper, which can then be mounted on black card and displayed against a bright background.

Reference to photocopiable sheets
The shape poems on photocopiable pages 154 and 155 should be used to stimulate discussion of the techniques involved in writing this kind of poem. Photocopiable page 156 should be cut into strips, so that each 'starter' can be given to a different child.

POETREE

To learn some of the key terms used in writing poetry and understand what they mean.

†† *Whole class, pairs, individual work, whole class.*

⏲ *50 minutes.*

Previous skills/knowledge needed
The children should be familiar with a range of different kinds of poetry, through both listening and reading. They should know that poems are usually made up of words in lines, and may use rhythm and rhyme. They should also be aware that poems can sometimes be written in the shape of the poem's subject.

Key background information
This activity is a 'word search' puzzle based on Mike Johnson's poem 'Poetree'. It encourages children to describe various features of poetry which are named in this poem: *line, verse, simile, image* and so on. The activity encourages close reading of the text, and also has a competitive element which will motivate many children to explore the poem in detail. It is important to note that concrete poems (see page 152) challenge some conventional notions of what a poem is.

Preparation
Make one A4 copy of photocopiable page 157 for each child. Make your own A3 copies (or OHP transparencies) of photocopiable pages 157 and 155. The latter was used in 'Shape poems' (page 108). It is well worth carrying out your own word search on the poem 'Poetree' (page 157): you will find more poetry terms every time you look at it!

Resources needed
Photocopiable pages 155 and 157; dictionaries; a board or flip chart; writing materials; anthologies or collections of poetry (see 'Suggestion(s) for support').

What to do
Gather the class together and tell them that you want them to tackle some detective work. Talk about detectives and how they need to search for hidden clues, using skill and patience. Like the heroes of television detective stories, the children must never give up. You might like to take a few minutes to listen to the children's favourite moments from current detective series.

Tell the children that their first task as 'poetry detectives' is to work out what makes a poem. Ask: *What makes a poem look different from other kinds of writing?* Elicit responses such as: *The words are usually written in lines. Sometimes the words rhyme. Poems are usually shorter than stories.* Use these responses to explore the elements of a poem, and how it differs from a work of prose.

Now show the children the A3 version of Mike Johnson's poem 'Poetree'. Ask them what it is. *A tree, a shape poem.* With no lines? *Yes, but it's still a poem.* What makes it a poem? *The words, the way they are written, the pattern they make on the page...* This discussion should help the children to realize that the word 'poem' is flexibly defined.

Tell the children that Mike Johnson's poem is a word search puzzle, and that their next task is to detect some of the poetry words hidden in it. Ask them to point out a few examples. They may well start with more obvious examples such as *words, poet* and *poem*. Scribe a few of these easy-to-find words on the flip chart.

Now give an A4 copy of 'Poetree' to each child, but tell them to work in pairs – detectives in films and TV series usually work with a 'partner' or 'buddy' (for example, Mulder

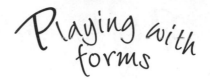

and Scully). Tell them that they can start with two of the words from the board, but that they should search for another four words at least. Allow five minutes for the pair to find and list as many words as they can. Point out that some of the words (such as *verse*) are bent around corners; and that sometimes one letter is used in more than one word, as in a crossword puzzle (for example, *pop* and *poem* on the top right-hand branch of the tree).

Use the children's responses to make a long list of 'poetry words' on the flip chart. Find out which of the words on this list the children know and understand. Underline these words, then set some of the children to look in dictionaries for the meanings of unfamiliar words. When they have done this, go over some of the more difficult terms with the children:

▲ *ballad*: a narrative poem in short stanzas;

▲ *simile*: where the poet says that something is *like* something else;

▲ *scan*: to make a poem fit a beat (or metre);

▲ *muse*: the mysterious inspiration for a poet's ideas;

▲ *metaphor*: when the poet says that something *is* something else;

▲ *poesy*: an old-fashioned word for poetry.

Most of the other terms will be familiar to the children: *verse, rhyme, rhythm, line, image, sentence* and so on.

Ask the children to work individually from their own poetry word lists to build their own *poetree*. They might add some words which Mike Johnson has missed out – for example: *stanza, metre, sonnet, limerick, haiku, alliteration* or *chorus*. Any words which are new to them should be checked in the dictionary. Encourage the children to draw a tree shape before they begin, and to use as many 'poetry words' as possible.

When they have finished, help the children to edit and correct their *poetrees* before writing them out in 'best' (see 'Display ideas' below).

Finally, gather the class back together and look at the A3 version of photocopiable page 156. Compare and contrast 'Poem' with 'Poetree'. Whereas 'Poetree' uses single words, 'Poem' uses phrases and whole sentences to describe what a poem is. Discuss the phrase 'as long as a piece of string', explaining what it means and when people might say it. Ask the children what other phrases they can find in this poem which say what a poem does.

Suggestions(s) for extension

More confident children could use anthologies and collections of poetry to find examples of the features referred to by some of the 'poetry words' which they have learnt. They could work as a group to copy out, annotate, cut and paste these extracts in a *Big Book About Poetry*, adding their own *poetree* poems. They could also make up a poem using a similar approach to that of 'Poem', expressing their own ideas about what a poem is.

Suggestion(s) for support

Children who need help can work with an adult to explore some children's poetry anthologies, looking for examples of such basic features as *line, verse, rhyme* and so on. The adult should scribe these 'finds' for the young detectives.

Assessment opportunities

Look for those children who know, understand and can use most of the technical terms used (at this level) in poetry-writing. Note those children who can construct a concrete poem in the *poetree* format.

Display ideas

When the children have edited their *poetree* poems, they can scribe them in 'best' using black ink on white paper. The *poetrees* could be roughly cut out and pasted on a sheet of black or dark brown backing paper, with each tree slightly overlapping or overlapped by its neighbours. This collage could be given the title *The Poetry Forest*.

Reference to photocopiable sheets

Photocopiable pages 155 and 157 should be enlarged to A3 size for display to the whole class during the lesson. A4 copies of page 157 should also be given to the children for closer examination. Page 155 was also used in the activity 'Shape poems' (see page 108).

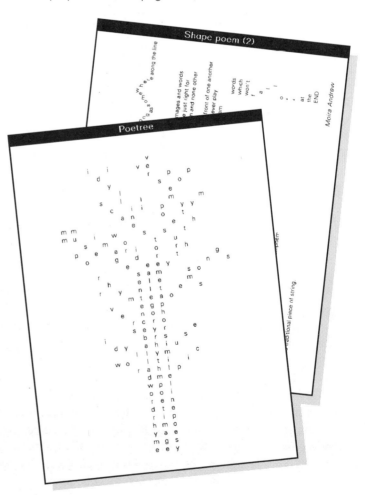

Photocopiables

The pages in this section can be photocopied for use in the classroom or school which has purchased this book, and do not need to be declared in any return in respect of any photocopying licence.

They comprise a varied selection of both pupil and teacher resources, including pupil worksheets, resource material and record sheets to be completed by the teacher or children. Most of the photocopiable pages are related to individual activities in the book; the name of the activity is indicated at the top of the sheet, together with a page reference indicating where the lesson plan for that activity can be found.

Individual pages are discussed in detail within each lesson plan, accompanied by ideas for adaptation where appropriate – of course, each sheet can be adapted to suit your own needs and those of your class. Sheets can also be coloured, laminated, mounted on to card, enlarged and so on where appropriate.

Pupil worksheets and record sheets have spaces provided for children's names and for noting the date on which each sheet was used. This means that, if so required, they can be included easily within any pupil assessment portfolio.

I got rhythm, I got rap, see page 20

Snap words

Tree	**Fun**	**Car**
Post	**Seen**	**Sing**
House	**Ball**	**Fly**
Said	**Sand**	**Food**
Rap	**Frock**	**Mill**
Din	**Top**	**Toy**

Photocopiables

I got rhythm, I got rap, see page 20

Snap pictures

Rhyme time, see page 24

Rhyming poems

Nursery rhyme updated

There was an old woman
who lived in a box.
She'd so few possessions
she'd no need for locks.
They gave her some soup
with two slices of bread,
then she wrapped up in rags,
made the pavement her bed.

Moira Andrew

No Excuses

I didn't do my homework Sir
I didn't hand it in,
it wasn't that I lost it Sir,
or dropped it in the bin.

It wasn't eaten up
by monsters out of space,
it wasn't that my baby brother
wiped it on his face.

It wasn't that our dog
chased it out the door,
it wasn't any of those things
you've heard ten times before.

It's just, I *didn't* do it Sir,
I know you think this strange,
only, I thought the truth Sir,
would make a lovely change.

Andrew Collett

Habits of the Hippopotamus

The hippopotamus is strong
And huge of head and broad of bustle;
The limbs on which he rolls along
Are big with hippopotomuscle.

He does not greatly care for sweets
Like ice-cream, apple pie, or custard,
But takes to flavour what he eats
A little hippopotomustard.

The hippopotamus is true
To all his principles, and just;
He always tries his best to do
The things one hippopotomust.

He never rides in trucks or trams,
In taxicabs or omnibuses,
And so keeps out of traffic jams
And other hippopotomusses.

Arthur Guiterman

Rhyme time, see page 24

More rhyming poems

Racing the wind

eyes staring
nostrils flaring

feet dancing
legs prancing

manes flowing
tails blowing

hooves pacing
horses racing

Moira Andrew

Biking

Fingers grip,
toes curl;
head down,
wheels whirl.

Hair streams,
fields race;
ears sting,
winds chase.

Breathe deep,
troubles gone;
just feel
windsong.

Judith Nicholls

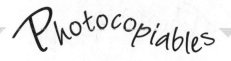
Tricky rhymes

Ocean	Outcrop	Defeat
Snowdrop	Swallow	Motion
Follow	Candle	Yellow
Fondle	Commotion	Retreat
Mellow	Describe	Palace
Tribe	Surface	Bombshell
Bluebell	Mountain	Fountain

The House on the Hill, see page 29

Reader beware

The House on the Hill

It was built years ago
by someone quite manic
and sends those who go there
away in blind panic.
They tell tales of horrors
that can injure or kill
designed by the madman
who lived on the hill.
    If you visit the House on the Hill for a dare
    remember my words...
           'There are dangers. Beware!'

The piano's white teeth
when you plonk out a note
will bite off your fingers
then reach for your throat.
The living-room curtains –
long, heavy and black –
will wrap you in cobwebs
if you're slow to step back.
    If you enter the House on the Hill for a dare
    remember my words...
           'There are dangers. Beware!'

The fridge in the kitchen
has a self-closing door.
If it knocks you inside
then you're ice cubes... for sure.
The steps to the cellar
are littered with bones,
and up from the darkness
drift creakings and groans.
    If you go to the House on the Hill for a dare
    remember my words...
           'There are dangers. Beware!'

Turn on the hot tap
and the bathroom will flood
not with gallons of water
but litres of blood.
The rocking-chair's arms
can squeeze you to death;
a waste of time shouting
as you run...out...of...breath.
    Don't say you weren't warned or told to take care
    when you entered the House on the Hill...
           for a dare.

Wes Magee

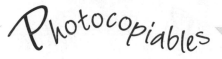

Family album, see page 32

A face from a family album

Portraits of summer, see page 35

Portraits of summer

Adlestrop

Yes, I remember Adlestrop –
The name, because one afternoon
Of heat the express-train drew up there
Unwontedly. It was late June.

The steam hissed. Someone cleared his throat.
No one left and no one came
On the bare platform. What I saw
Was Adlestrop – only the name

And willows, willow-herb, and grass,
And meadow sweet, and haycocks dry,
No whit less still and lonely fair
Than the high cloudlets in the sky.

And for that minute a blackbird sang
Close by, and round him, mistier,
Farther and farther, all the birds
Of Oxfordshire and Gloucestershire.

Edward Thomas

from **Rain in summer**

How beautiful is the rain!
After the dust and heat,
In the broad and fiery street,
In the narrow lane,
How beautiful is the rain!

How it clatters along the roofs,
Like the tramp of hoofs!
How it gushes and struggles out
From the throat of the overflowing spout!

Across the window-pane
It pours and pours;
And swift and wide,
With a muddy tide,
Like a river down the gutter roars
The rain, the welcome rain!

H.W. Longfellow

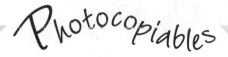
Tell me a story, see page 38

Story poem (1)

The *Alice Jean*

One moonlight night a ship drove in,
　A ghostly ship from the west,
Drifting with bare mast and lone tiller;
　Like a mermaid drest
In long green weed and barnacles
　She beached and came to rest.

All the watchers of the coast
　Flocked to view the sight;
Men and women, streaming down
　Through the summer night.
Found her standing tall and ragged
　Beached in the moonlight.

Then one old woman stared aghast:
　'The *Alice Jean*? But no!
The ship that took my Ned from me
　Sixty years ago –
Drifted back from the utmost west
　With the ocean's flow?

'Caught and caged in the weedy pool
　Beyond the western brink,
Where crewless vessels lie and rot
　In waters black as ink,
Torn out at last by a sudden gale –
　Is it the *Jean*, you think?'

A hundred women gaped at her,
　The menfolk nudged and laughed,
But none could find a likelier story
　For the strange craft
With fear and death and desolation
　Rigged fore and aft.

The blind ship came forgotten home
　To all but one of these,
Of whom none dared to climb aboard her:
　And by and by the breeze
Veered hard about, and the *Alice Jean*
　Foundered in foaming seas.

Robert Graves

Tell me a story, see page 38

Story poem (2)

The apple-raid

Darkness came early, though not yet cold;
Stars were strung on the telegraph wires;
Street lamps spilled pools of liquid gold;
The breeze was spiced with garden fires.

The smell that burnt leaves, the early dark,
Can still excite me but not as it did
So long ago when we met in the Park –
Myself, John Peters and David Kidd.

We moved out of town to the district where
The lucky and wealthy had their homes
With garages, gardens, and apples to spare
Ripely clustered in the trees' green domes.

We chose the place we meant to plunder
And climbed the wall and dropped down to
The secret dark. Apples crunched under
Our feet as we moved through the grass and dew.

The clusters on the lower boughs of the tree
Were easy to reach. We stored the fruit
In pockets and jerseys until all three
Boys were heavy with their tasty loot.

Safe on the other side of the wall
We moved back to town and munched as we went.
I wonder if David remembers at all
That little adventure, the apples' fresh scent?

Strange to think that he's fifty years old,
That tough little boy with scabs on his knees;
Stranger to think that John Peters lies cold
In an orchard in France beneath apple trees.

Vernon Scannell

Tell me a story, see page 38

Story poem (3)

Act of worship

Every Sunday morning my grandmother
should have won a medal for bravery.
Every Sunday she dressed in her best,
walked to church on Grandfather's arm.

They sat upstairs in the front pew
high above hats and nodding heads,
she in fur tippet, he in navy Sunday
suit, gold watch chain, topaz fob.

Every Sunday they stood up to sing.
No head for heights, Gran jammed the
back of her knees against the seat,
her fine contralto faint with fear.

Sick, dizzy, she dared not look down.
'Why not tell him?' I asked. 'Oh no,'
she said. 'Your grandfather says it's
the place to be. I'll get used to it.'

But she never did. She would produce
peppermints from a paper bag, hand
them round, part of the weekly ritual.
Grandfather bowed to acquaintances below.

Moira Andrew

Tell me a story, see page 38

Story poem (4)

Miller's End

When we moved to Miller's End,
    Every afternoon at four
A thin shadow of a shade
    Quavered through the garden-door.

Dressed in black from top to toe
    And a veil about her head
To us all it seemed as though
    She came walking from the dead.

With a basket on her arm
    Through the hedge-gap she would pass,
Never a mark that we could spy
    On the flagstones or the grass.

When we told the garden-boy
    How we saw the phantom glide,
With a grin his face was bright
    As the pool he stood beside.

'That's no ghost-walk,' Billy said,
    'Nor a ghost you fear to stop –
Only old Miss Wickerby
    On a short cut to the shop.'

So next day we lay in wait,
    Passed a civil time of day,
Said how pleased we were she came
    Daily down our garden-way.

Suddenly her cheek it paled,
    Turned, as quick, from ice to flame.
'Tell me,' said Miss Wickerby.
    'Who spoke of me, and my name?'

'Bill the garden-boy.'
                    She sighed,
    Said, 'Of course, you could not know
How he drowned – that very pool –
    A frozen winter – long ago.'

Charles Causley

Old Jack Rags, see page 41

A poem for discussion

Sunlight or surprise?

No, don't go near him, people say,
He's full of fleas, so keep away
From Old Jack Rags.

He's never tidy, never clean,
The filthiest tramp you've ever seen,
Is Old Jack Rags.

He lives on rubbish, sleeps in dirt,
He's only got one grubby shirt,
Has Old Jack Rags.

His teeth are black, his eyes are red,
He eats small children with his bread,
Does Old Jack Rags.

No, don't go near him, people say,
But I went near, just yesterday,
To Old Jack Rags

And: 'Do you sleep in dirt?' I said,
'And eat small children with your bread?
Well, Old Jack Rags?'

Then was it sunlight or surprise
That made those tears start from the eyes
Of Old Jack Rags?

Richard Edwards

One-parent family, see page 44

A character poem

One-parent family

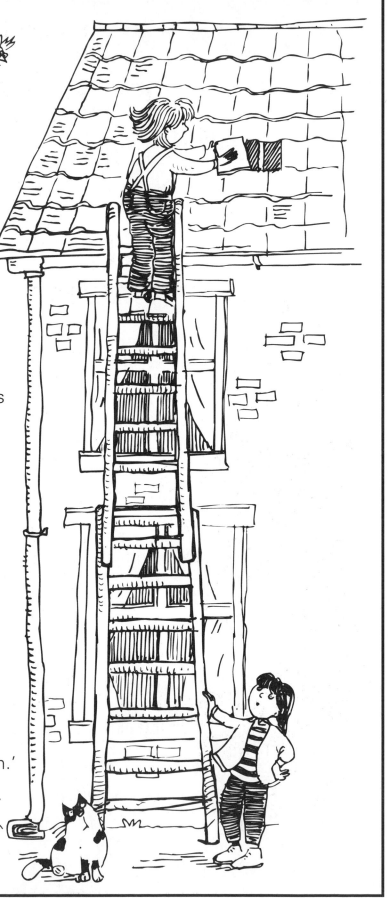

My mum says she's clueless
not, as you'd imagine,
at wiring three-pin plugs or
straightening a bicycle wheel,
but at sewing buttons
on a shirt, icing names and
dates on birthday cakes,
preparing a three-course meal.

She's not like other mothers;
although she's slim and neat
she looks silly in an apron,
just great in dungarees.
She'll tackle any household job,
lay lino, fix on tiles, does
all the outside paintwork, climbs
a ladder with practised ease.

Mind you, she's good for
a cuddle when I fall and
cut my knee. She tells me
fantastic stories every night,
laughs at *my* disasters, says
that she's as bad when she
reads a recipe all wrong and
her cakes don't come out right.

I know on Open Evenings
she gives a bad impression
at the school. She doesn't wear
the proper clothes. 'Too bad,'
the others sometimes say,
'you've got such a peculiar mum.'
'It's just as well,' I tell them.
'She is my mother *and* my dad!'

Moira Andrew

Images of the moon, see page 48

A moon poem

Moon thoughts

The moon is a ripe pumpkin
waiting for Hallowe'en teeth.

It is a yellow gumdrop
sucked enough to see through.

It is a slice of lemon
souring a ginger beer sky.

It is an antique Hunter watch
worn across night's stomach.

It is a brass button lost
from some sailor's pea jacket.

The moon is far enough away
to fantasise about, despite

Apollo and man's long steps.

Moira Andrew

Images of the moon, see page 48

Writing frame

The moon

The moon _____

like a _____

_____

like a _____

_____

like a _____

_____

like a _____

_____

like a _____

_____

like a _____

By _____

A poem is..., see page 51

A poem is...

A poem is _____

_____

It is _____

_____

Christmas is _____

_____

It is _____

_____

Night is _____

_____

It is _____

_____

School is _____

_____

It is _____

_____

Don't!

Don't _____

_____

Don't _____

_____   by _____

What can I do with it?, see page 56

A list poem (1)

What Can You Do With A Pencil?

(For an unknown boy in Winchester)

You can sharpen it
or break the point,
trap it in the door;
fasten it behind your ear
or *tap* it on the floor;
use it as a walking stick
(if you're very small),
dig a hole to plant a seed,
tap it on a wall;
use it as a handy splint
for rabbits' broken legs;
stir your coffee,
stir your tea,
stir up all the dregs!
Drop it from a table top,
pop it in a case;
use it as a lollystick,
send it up in space!
Two will give you chopsticks,
one could pick a lock;
bore a hole and thread one
to darn a hole-y sock...

These are just a few ideas,
there must be *hundreds* more...
but meantime, trap it, snap it, flap it,

TAP IT ON THE FLOOR!

Judith Nicholls

What can I do with it?, see page 56

A list poem (2)

Ten things to do with a frisbee

You can spin it in the air.
You can whizz it across a chair.

You can send it into space.
You can enter it in a race.

You can fly it above the trees.
You can float it on the breeze.

You can zip it across the sky.
You can make it soar up very high.

You can fling it over the river.
Help! You've lost track of it forever!

Moira Andrew

What can I do with it?, see page 56

A secret poem

by ——————————————

What's my secret?

Fold

Fold

What's my secret?

——————————————

——————————————

——————————————

——————————————

——————————————

——————————————

Lift the flap to
find out.

A river of words, see page 59

A river of words

Stone	Waterfall	Forest
Sun	Seashore	Motorway
River	Stars	Space
Underwater	Mountain	School
Holiday	Rooftop	Pathway
Gate	Garden	Magic
Home	Light	Sleep
Night	Photograph	Street
Train	Soap	Hands
Tears	Morning	Dustbin

Beachcomber, see page 62

A poem about a 'found' object

A driftwood pendant

Sandpaper off
the roughness, rub
away the patina
that sand and sea
have left.

Remove the blemishes,
but carefully
retain the basic form
that sand and sea
have given it.

Consider what the sea
would work on it next;
search out soft surfaces;
erode them gently:
be the sea.

Accentuate
the forms that interest;
subtly impose
intelligence
the sea could not.

Smooth down the whole.
Follow the grain;
refine each surface
equally. Return
again, again.

Next use a seal
to bring out colour
and preserve; when dry,
sandpaper lightly
and repeat.

The final stages: bore
a careful hole,
soften a thong,
thread it, and knot.
Now find a girl.

John Loveday

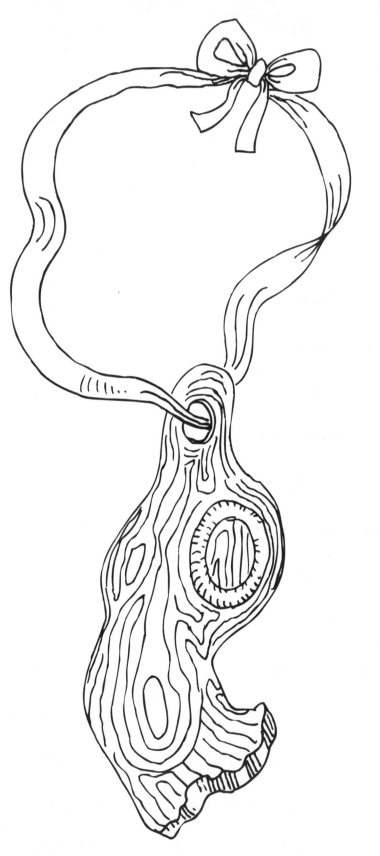

Beachcomber, see page 62

Treasure island

by _____

A 'found' poem

Raspberry jam

Take 4lbs of fruit.
Use whole clean berries.
Gran's script, the colour
of tea, loops its advice
across a blue-lined pad.

On summer afternoons
we ease ripe berries
from their canes,
heaping them fragrant
into a great glass bowl.

Put in pan. Add 4 lbs.
preserving sugar. Bring
slowly to the boil.
We follow instructions,
stirring in turn.

Keep to a full rolling
boil for five minutes
only. Pot up. The
heaving mass is pocked
with seed, darkens.

Just five minutes. No
more. We let it cool,
pot up into heated jars.
4 + 4 fills 9 pots! Gran's
jam defies the rules.

Moira Andrew

I've found a poem! see page 65

Newspaper headlines

THE WOODLAND GAZETTE

Danger – children at risk

_____
_____
_____
_____
_____
_____
_____

Frost and snow blankets hills

_____
_____
_____
_____
_____
_____
_____
_____
_____
_____
_____
_____

_____
_____
_____
_____

Coldest night on record

_____
_____
_____
_____
_____

Do not drive unless you have to

_____
_____
_____
_____
_____
_____

Wonderland scene in forest

_____
_____
_____
_____

Box of dreams, see page 68

A box for a poem

Box of

by

_____

_____

_____

_____

_____

_____

_____

_____

King am I! see page 73

A magical poem

The paint box

'Cobalt and umber and ultramarine,
Ivory black and emerald green –
What shall I paint to give pleasure to you?'
'Paint for me somebody utterly new.'

'I have painted you tigers in crimson and white.'
'The colours were good and you painted aright.'
'I have painted the cook and a camel in blue
And a panther in purple.' 'You painted them true.

Now mix me a colour that nobody knows,
And paint me a country where nobody goes,
And put in it people a little like you,
Watching a unicorn drinking the dew.'

E.V. Rieu

Through that door, see page 78

A rhyming poem in verses

Through that door

Through that door
Is a garden with a wall,
The red brick crumbling,
The lupins growing tall,
Where the lawn is like a carpet
Spread for you,
And it's all as tranquil
As you never knew.

Through that door
Is the great ocean-sea
Which heaves and rolls
To eternity,
With its islands and promontories
Waiting for you
To explore and discover
In that vastness of blue.

Through that door
Is your secret room
Where the window lets in
The light of the moon,
With its mysteries and magic
Where you can find
Thrills and excitements
Of every kind.

Through that door
Are the mountains and the moors
And the rivers and the forests
Of the great outdoors,
All the plains and the ice-caps
And lakes as blue as sky
For all those creatures
That walk or swim or fly.

Through that door
Is the city of the mind
Where you can imagine
What you'll find.
You can make of that city
What you want it to,
And if you choose to share it,
Then it could come true.

John Cotton

If I were an artist, see page 80

If I were an artist

Portrait of a Dragon

If I were an artist
I'd paint the portrait
of a dragon.

To do a proper job
I'd borrow colours
from the world.

For his back I'd
need a mountain range,
all misty-blue.

For spikes I'd use
dark fir trees pointing
to the sky.

For overlapping scales
I'd squeeze dye from
bright anemones.

I'd gild his claws
like shining swords
with starlight.

His tail would be
a river, silver
in the sun.

For his head, the
secret green of forests
and deep seas.

And his eyes would
glow like embers in
a tinker's fire.

But I'd keep the best
till last. For his
hot breath

I'd use all reds and
yellows – crocus, saffron,
peony, poppy,

geranium, cyclamen, rose -
and fierce orange flames
from a marigold.

Moira Andrew

If I were an artist, see page 80

Writing frame

Portrait of a unicorn

For his head

I'd use a _____

_____

For his body

I'd have a _____

_____

For his hooves

I'd borrow _____

_____

For his tail

I'd use a _____

_____

And for his horn

I'd need a _____

_____

by _____

Above and beyond, see page 82

Poetic prepositions

Beyond my house

Above my house
is the blue of the sky,
fragile fishbone clouds
and the wind whispering
    like an untold wish.

Below my house
is the dark secret earth,
deep-spiralling roots
and the mystery of lives
    lived underground.

Around my house
is the garden wall, where
slow snails crawl and spiders
hang their webs, beaded
    like door curtains.

Beside my house
is an apple tree, a
shady place to hide
in summer, in winter
    a bony skeleton.

Over my house
is a rainbow, a magic
paint-splashed bridge
where raindrops shine
    like crystal beads.

Inside my house
is my family, my laughing,
crying, quarrelling family,
a place where I belong
    every single day.

Beyond my house
is the future, full of promise
as an unopened parcel
wrapped in fancy paper
    and silver ribbons.

Moira Andrew

Above and beyond, see page 82

Writing frame

Above my house

Above my house

is _____

_____

_____

Beside my house

is _____

_____

_____

Below my house

is _____

_____

_____

by _____

Inside my head, see page 84

Inside my head

Night

There's a dark, dark wood
inside my head
where the night owl cries;
where clambering roots
catch at my feet
where fox and bat
and badger meet
and night has eyes.

There's a dark, dark wood
inside my head
of oak and ash and pine;
where the clammy grasp
of a beaded web
can raise the hairs
on a wanderer's head
as he stares alone
from his mossy bed
and feels
the chill of his spine.

There's a dark, dark wood
inside my head
where the spider weaves;
where the rook rests
and the pale owl nests,
where moonlit bracken
spikes the air
and the moss is covered,
layer upon layer,
by a thousand fallen leaves.

Judith Nicholls

Recipe for summer, see page 88

Writing frame

Recipe for summer

Take _____

_____

and _____

Add _____

_____

and _____

Mix _____

_____

and _____

_____

and _____

Bake _____

_____

and you have made summer!

by _____

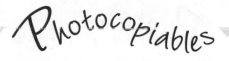

Alphabet poems, see page 90

Animal alphabet

a _____ _____ _____

b _____ _____ _____

c _____ _____ _____

d _____ _____ _____

e _____ _____ _____

f _____ _____ _____

g _____ _____ _____

h _____ _____ _____

i _____ _____ _____

j _____ _____ _____

k _____ _____ _____

l _____ _____ _____

m _____ _____ _____

n _____ _____ _____

o _____ _____ _____

p _____ _____ _____

q _____ _____ _____

r _____ _____ _____

s _____ _____ _____

t _____ _____ _____

u _____ _____ _____

v _____ _____ _____

w _____ _____ _____

x x-cellent xemas x-celling

y _____ _____ _____

z _____ _____ _____

POETRY

A letter poem

Letter from Egypt

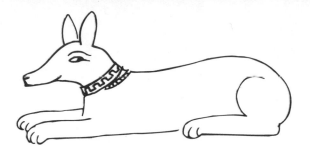

Dear Miriam,
    Just a line
to let you know how things
are with us & of course to
thank you (& your good man)
for all you did for us – &
at your busiest time too
what with the census &
everything. I was quite
exhausted & and the baby was
beginning to make himself
felt. If it hadn't been
for your help that night
my baby might have died.

    Good of you
to put up with all our
visitors – who'd have
thought, six scruffy
shepherds up & leaving
their sheep like that?
& didn't they ever smell?
Still they were good-
hearted & they meant well.
I hope they brought some
extra trade to the inn.
They looked in need of
a hot drink & a meal.

    & what about
those Kings, Miriam? Kneeling
there in their rich robes
& all? & me in nothing but
my old blue dress! Joseph
said not to worry, it was
Jesus they'd come to see.
Real gentlemen *they* were.
But what funny things to
give a baby – gold & myrrh
& frankincense. That's men
all over! It wouldn't cross
their minds to bring a shawl!

    Sorry we left
so suddenly. No time for
good-byes with King Herod on
the warpath! We had to take
the long way home & I'm so
tired of looking at sand!
Joseph has picked up a few
jobs mending this & that so
we're managing quite well.
Jesus grows bonnier every
day & thrives on this way
of life, but I can't wait
to see Nazareth again.

Love to all
at the inn,

Mary

Moira Andrew

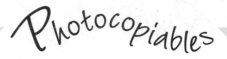

Riddles, see page 100

Traditional riddles

A wee wee man
in a red red coat,
a stick in his hand
and a stone in his throat.
What is he?

White bird, featherless,
Flew from Paradise,
Pitched on the castle wall;
Along came the Princess,
Took it up handless,
Rode away horseless to the King's white hall.
What was the weather?

Riddle me, riddle me, what is that,
Over your head and under your hat?

White sheep, white sheep,
On a blue hill.
When the wind stops
You all stand still.
What are you?

Acrostics, see page 104

Three acrostic poems

CHRISTMAS

Carol-singing in the frosty air,
Holly wreaths all down the stair.
Reindeer galloping across the night,
Ivy looped with tinsel bright.
Stockings hung on ends of beds,
Trees dressed up in golds and reds.
Mince pies ready, spiced and hot,
A baby in a manger cot.
Stars to guide kings all the way........
.... And we wake up to Christmas Day!

SEPTEMBER

Sunshine still painting the sky,
Each rudbeckia still reaching high,
Petals still clinging to the flowers,
Trees still bending beneath the showers,
Every apple still hanging aloft,
Moss still damp and green and soft.
Birds still gathering on telephone wires,
Everyone still cooking on barbecue fires,
Real autumn weather is still on hold,

but as September fades, the days grow cold.

OCTOBER

O for the owls that call from the night,
C for the crows fast-flying out of sight,
T for the trees that are shedding their leaves,
O for the oak as for summer it grieves,
B for the berries so sweet and so black,
E for the elms that wither and crack,
R for the robins who always come back.

Autumn the season that lets in the cold,
OCTOBER the month when the year grows old.

all by Moira Andrew

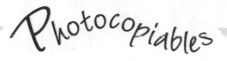
Acrostics of the seasons

S _____

P _____

R _____

I _____

N _____

G _____

S _____

U _____

M _____

M _____

E _____

R _____

A _____

U _____

T _____

U _____

M _____

N _____

W _____

I _____

N _____

T _____

E _____

R _____

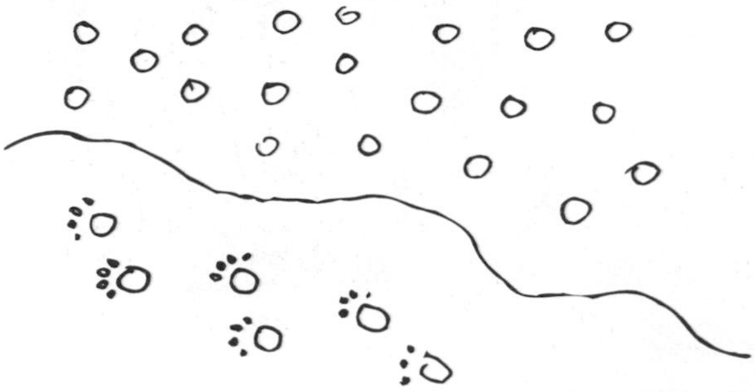

by _____

Sequences, see page 106

A sequence poem

Sea seasons

The sea bounces
over barnacles,
bobbing and buckling
in the springtime breeze.

The sea slithers
across shingle,
splintering and sparkling
under a bright summer sun.

The sea prowls
over pebbles,
pimpling and prickling
on damp autumn days.

The sea rushes
across rocks,
ranting and raving
when winter winds blow.

Moira Andrew

Shape poem (1)

Snake
Snake slithers
    among stones,
        coils and loops
            and hisses
            forked tongue
        darts as fast
as an arrow,
    aims and misses.

Snake glides
    over pebbles,
        sleeps, snoozing
            in the sun,
            hunger long-
        forgotten,
waits still, till
    day is done.

Moira Andrew

Shape poem (2)

Poem

A poem is like a step ladder
it sometimes seems to me

You go up to the roof to make your point and

A poem can do
its work for you
when it just

m e a n d e r s in and out of ideas as l o n g as s o m e h e r e along the line

it uses images and words
which are just right for
that poem and none other

words which belong behind and in front of one another
in an exact order and which could never play
follow-my-leader in any different poem

words
which
won't
f
a l
l
o
f
f
at
the
END

down again, stepping
carefully on each word.

Or occasionally it's
a strong tight rope
anchoring your thoughts to the deck poempoempoe
mpoempoempo
empoempoemp
oempoempoem

It can be as
short
or as long as the traditional piece of string.

Moira Andrew

Poetree, see page 108

Images for starters

Stars glittering like _____

_____

Waves crashing like_____

_____

Clouds floating like _____

_____

The wind blowing like _____

_____

Mist creeping like _____

_____

The moon shining like _____

_____

A river twisting like _____

_____

A worm wriggling like_____

_____

A volcano smoking like _____

_____

Poetree, see page 111

Poetree

```
                        v
      i     i       v   e     p     p
        d             r     p   o
          y         s       e   o
            l             e m       m
      s       l     l     p   y   y
        c       i     i   p       
          a       n     o     e     h
m m         e           s     t
m u     i     w       s     s     t
  s   m       o           t     u
    p   e       a   r   i   o   r   h
      o       g       d   o   r   t       g
              e       e   e   y       n       s
          r         s   a   m       s   o
            h       e   l   e     m
          r     y   n   l   t   e     s
              m   t   e   a   o
                v   e   g   o
                  e   n   o   r
                      c   r   o
                      s   e   y
                      i     b   r   s     s
                        d   y   a   h   i   u
                            l   l   y   m     c
                      w   o   l   t   i     i
                            r   a   h   l   p
                                d   m   e
                                w   p   l
                                o   o   i
                                r   e   n
                                d   t   e
                                r   i   p
                                h   m   o
                                y   a   e
                                m   g   s
                                e   e   y
```

INFORMATION TECHNOLOGY AND POETRY AT KEY STAGE 2

The main emphasis for the development of IT capability within these activities is on communicating information, particularly through the use of word processing software.

Word processing

Many of the poetry writing activities in this book can be used to develop children's IT capability through the use of a word processor. The teacher could organize children to do different writing tasks over a term or longer, some using more conventional written methods and others using the computer. This would allow the teacher to provide activities at different levels of IT capability, and to discuss with different children the relative merits of the use of IT for different purposes.

During Key Stage 2, pupils should be developing their confidence and competence in using word processing or desktop publishing (DTP) packages. Many word processors now have basic DTP features, and it may be possible to use a single piece of software for most writing tasks. A key difference between the two types of software is the way in which text is placed on the page. In a DTP package, text is generally placed inside a frame which can be altered in size and shape; the text is automatically reformatted to fill the new shape. This provides a flexible way for children to organize text and pictures on a page, and to experiment with different types of page design.

Children should already have a basic knowledge of the keyboard, and should be given opportunities to use some of the more sophisticated aspects of a word processor or DTP package. They should be able to:

▲ use more than one finger per hand when typing, particularly once they know where the letters are;
▲ separate and join text using the *return* and *delete* keys;
▲ move the cursor to a mistake and correct it without deleting all the text back to the mistake;
▲ scroll around the document using the mouse or keys;
▲ select an appopriate font from a menu;
▲ change the size and/or colour of a font;
▲ underline a word or line;
▲ alter the style of a word or sentence to *italic* or **bold**;
▲ centre text using the *centre* command;
▲ use the *tab* key to position text and create columns;
▲ set and reset right/left and fully justified text;
▲ save their work to disk and retrieve it;
▲ print out their work independently;
▲ use a spelling checker and an electronic thesaurus;
▲ add pictures to their work and position and resize them.
Older or more able children should be able to:
▲ alter the 'ruler' to change margins and set Tab keys;

▲ use the word-count facility;
▲ insert page numbers;
▲ set up a master page to create a consistent layout throughout a document;
▲ set up a text style to use within a document.

Children should be given opportunities to originate their work at the computer keyboard, rather than only using a word processor to make a 'fair copy'. It is often appropriate for children to make their first draft at the keyboard, save it, print it out and then redraft it away from the keyboard, giving another child the opportunity to use the computer. They can then retrieve their work later, edit it and format the final copy for printing.

Many of these activities suggest the use of word-processed files created in advance by the teacher. This will enable children to concentrate on their poetry writing skills, or on the more sophisticated word-processing commands of editing, organizing and presenting work. When such files are created, it is important to make sure that a backup is kept or that the 'master' file is locked against accidental overwriting when children save their own versions.

When activities involve moving text around the page, the use of the 'cut and paste' facility (or the 'drag and drop' facility, where appropriate) should be taught. A useful idea for drafting on screen is to put extra words or phrases at the bottom of a poem, so that they can be picked up and added later.

Children should be shown how to use an electronic thesaurus. This may come as part of the word processor, so that children can highlight a word and then search for alternatives. Some computers may have a dedicated thesaurus apart from the word processor; it may come on a CD-ROM, or be loaded onto the hard drive. A versatile alternative comes as part of a hand-held, portable thesaurus; often this is part of a spelling package.

Where teachers have access to a large monitor or computer projector, they can use a word processor instead of a flip chart to show children how drafting can be achieved at the computer. As more primary schools have access to a computer room, this facility may become more widely available.

Publishing work on the Internet

As more schools have access to the Internet and create their own World Wide Web pages, it will be possible for children to place their poetry on the Internet, encouraging children from other schools to comment on them or contribute their own poems. Where schools have e-mail links to partner schools, they could send copies of their poems to pen pals or other classes. The poems should be sent as part of an e-mail message, as an attached file in plain or ASCII text (which has no formatting commands), or as an attached word-processed file. The schools will need to agree on a common file format.

The grids on this page relate the activities in this Curriculum Bank to specific areas of IT and to relevant software resources. The activities are referenced by page number. Bold page numbers indicate activities which have expanded IT content (in relation to a specific area of IT). The software listed is a selection of programs generally available to primary schools, and is not intended as a recommended list. The software programs featured should be available from most good educational software retailers.

AREA OF IT	SOFTWARE	ACTIVITIES (page nos.)			
		CH. 1	CH. 2	CH. 3	CH. 4
Communicating information	Word processor	18, 24, 27, 29, 32, 35, 41	48, 51, 54, 59, **62,** 68, 70	78, 80, 82, **84,** 88, 90, 92	96, **98,** 103, 106, 108
Communicating information	DTP	29	54, 70	82	106
Communicating information	Art package	18, 29	51, 54, 62, 68, 73	78, 80, 84	
Communicating information	Drawing package	29	62, 68	78, 84	108
Communicating information	Authoring software	**24**, 35	56, 62		**100**
Information handling	Internet			92	
Control	Tape recorder	20, 35, 41			

SOFTWARE TYPE	BBC/MASTER	RISCOS	NIMBUS/186	WINDOWS	MACINTOSH
Word Processor	Folio	Pendown Desk Top Folio Textease	All Write Write On	Word Write Away Textease Claris Works	Word Easy Works Claris Works Creative Writer
DTP		Pendown DTP Ovation Textease		PagePlus Publisher Textease	
Art package	Picture Builder	1st Paint Kid Pix Dazzle	Picture Builder	Colour Magic Kid Pix 2 Microsoft Paint Dazzle	Kid Pix 2 Microsoft Paint Claris Works
Multi-media authoring package		Magpie Hyperstudio Genesis Textease		Genesis Hyperstudio Illuminatus Textease	Hyperstudio
Drawing package	Picture Builder	Draw Picture IT Art Works	Picture Builder	Claris Works Microsoft Draw	Claris Works Microsoft Draw

	SCIENCE	GEOGRAPHY	HISTORY	ART	MUSIC	D&T	IT	RE/PSE
LISTENING AND READING	Discussing butterflies and their habitats; referring to natural history books. Discussing family resemblance and the ageing process. Looking at the weather and wildlife of summer.		Exploring the historical context of poems from the past.	Drawing butterflies with realistic wing patterns. Drawing a story in 'comic strip' format. Making cut-out silhouette images. Making a frieze.	Clapping out the rhythms in a 'rap' lyric. Using an electronic keyboard to create a beat. Being aware of rhyme as a musical effect.	Making a concertina book. Making a large floor book.	Using an art package to create symmetrical pictures. Using a word processor to write, edit and design text. Adding clip art or scanned drawings to a page. Using art software to create or enhance images. Using multi-media authoring software. Using a DTP package to create a newspaper page. Using a tape recorder.	Discussing 'ghostly' themes and experiences of fear (in a non-threatening context). Thinking about social attitudes and prejudices. Understanding the feelings of isolated people. Discussing different kinds of 'family'.
WRITING POEMS	Exploring ideas about the moon. Looking at seasonal contrasts in nature. Exploring the senses.	Researching war and famine.		Making friezes of various kinds.	Considering the moods suggested by pieces of music in terms of colours. Considering the rhythm or beat of a poem.	Making a 'moons' mobile. Inventing new uses for familiar objects. Looking at instructions for practical tasks.	See above. Using an electronic thesaurus. Using an art package with colour blending or washes; using a colour palette. Using different font colours and shades. Using the 'cut and paste' facility on a word processor. Using an OCR scanner. Taking text from a CD-ROM. Combining text and artwork on screen. Working from a given text file.	Discussing the effects of war and famine. Contrasting creative power and political power.
USING A PATTERN	Learning the names of various animals.	Considering different kinds of landscape. Looking at buildings in the local environment and elsewhere. Discussing means of communication over distance.	Adapting the viewpoint of a character from history.	Creating designs based on the imaginative use of real shapes. Making friezes with three-dimensional features.		Displaying a poem behind an opening 'door'. Making a pictorial frame for a poem.	See above. Corresponding with other children via e-mail.	Thinking about the Nativity story from the mother's viewpoint.
PLAYING WITH FORMS	Exploring the vocabulary of fire and burning. Looking at the weather and natural features associated with each month of the year. Looking at the seasons as a pattern.			Drawing and colouring letters in an 'illuminated script' style. Creating pictorial shape poems.		Making a zigzag book. Making a layered mobile.	See above. Taking photographs with a digital camera and adding them to text on screen. Using clip art fonts to make simple illuminated letters. Using a word processor or a drawing package to design a shape poem.	